ROUTLEDGE LIBRARY EDITIONS: DEVELOPMENT

IMAGES AND BEHAVIOR OF PRIVATE BANK LENDING TO DEVELOPING COUNTRIES

IMAGES AND BEHAVIOR OF PRIVATE BANK LENDING TO DEVELOPING COUNTRIES

MARGEE M. ENSIGN

Volume 14

Routledge
Taylor & Francis Group
LONDON AND NEW YORK

First published in 1988

This edition first published in 2011 by Routledge

Published 2014 by Routledge
2 Park Square, Milton Park, Abingdon, Oxfordshire OX14 4RN

Simultaneously published in the USA and Canada
by Routledge
711 Third Avenue, New York, NY 10017 USA

First issued in paperback 2014

Routledge is an imprint of the Taylor & Francis Group, an informa business

British Library Cataloguing in Publication Data
A catalogue record for this book is available from the British Library

ISBN 13: 978-0-415-58414-2 (Set)
ISBN 13: 978-0-415-59279-6 (Volume 14)
ISBN13: 978-1-138-86564-8 (pbk)

Publisher's Note

The publisher has gone to great lengths to ensure the quality of this reprint but points out that some imperfections in the original copies may be apparent.

Disclaimer

The publisher has made every effort to trace copyright holders and welcomes correspondence from those they have been unable to contact.

IMAGES AND BEHAVIOR OF PRIVATE BANK LENDING TO DEVELOPING COUNTRIES

By Margee M. Ensign
Columbia University

Gordon and Breach Science Publishers
New York London Paris Montreux Tokyo Melbourne

Gordon and Breach Science Publishers

Post Office Box 786
Cooper Station
New York, New York 10276
United States of America

Post Office Box 197
London WC2E 9PX
England

58, rue Lhomond
75005 Paris
France

3-14-9, Okubo
Shinjuku-ku, Tokyo
Japan

Private Bag 8
Camberwell, Victoria 3124
Australia

Library of Congress Cataloging-in-Publication Data

Ensign, Margee M., 1954–
Images and behavior of private bank lending to developing countries / Margee M. Ensign.
p. cm.
Bibliography: p.
Includes index.
ISBN 2-88124-290-1
1. Loans, Foreign—Developing countries. 2. Banks and banking—Developing countries. I. Title.
HG3891.5.E57 1988 332.1'5—dc19 88-11313

CONTENTS

ACKNOWLEDGMENTS

Many individuals have contributed to the research contained in this book. I would like to especially thank my former professors at the University of Maryland, Warren R. Phillips and Cheryl Christensen, who provided the initial inspiration for the methodological approach, my first tutor in international politics, Margaret Bates of New College, and Peter deLeon of the University of Colorado for insightful comments. This book could not have been completed without the intellectual and emotional support of my husband, Alan R. Aronson, and my parents, Margaret and Richard Ensign. To them I dedicate this book.

The U.S. banks do not appear to have dashed with abandon into LDC commitments. The Banker, 1977.

INTRODUCTION

The relationship between private commercial banks and borrowers in the developing countries has generated a great deal of controversy. In recent years the literature on the debt problems of the developing countries has increased almost as rapidly as the debt itself. Much of this literature has focused on the scope of the problem, the vulnerability of the banks involved in lending to developing countries and the potential threat to the international monetary system[1] or on the impact of debt on development.

The debt problem is a major dilemma for both the developing and the industrialized countries. The external debt of all developing countries has grown from $448.0 billion in 1980 to over $700 billion in 1986, [2] (See Figure One). The larger borrowers have been primarily the middle income developing countries, [3], particularly the Latin America countries, and major lenders have been the large U.S. banks. The ten major Latin American debtors alone owed $346.3 billion as of mid-1985; [4] $70 billion of this is owed to the U.S. banks.

While a great deal has been learned about the debt problem, one area is not well understood: that is how the banks made decisions on the creditworthiness of the less-developed countries (LDC's). This study examines the lending behavior of six U.S. banks when one of these banks was the lead bank in a syndicated loan made in the Eurocurrency market.

The primary questions addressed by this study are: how did U.S. bankers make decisions on the creditworthiness of developing countries during the 1970's; what are the implications of these decision rules for the developing countries, and can these decisions rules or images of creditworthiness give us any clues about the prospects for renewed lending by the private banks.

Several important developments in international financial markets, particularly the rise of syndicated loans, provided the structural foundation for private bank loans to the developing countries during the 1970's. These innovations, along with the changing international lending environment of the 1970's, are analyzed in chapter two.

During the early period of lending to the developing countries in the 1970's, U.S. bankers did not have elaborate statistical information on these borrowers. Instead these bankers often relied on subjective perceptions in making judgments on creditworthiness. These subjective perceptions were formalized into a set of decision rules or algorithms and incorporated into artificial-intelligence based simulations. The results of simulations were compared to empirical data on loans, spreads and country characteristics to see if the bankers' images of creditworthiness matched their lending behavior. The methodology underlying the simulations is presented in chapter three.

The relationship between the bankers' images of creditworthiness and the lending behavior is presented in chapter four along with a discussion of the implications of the

relationship for the developing countries.
The analysis suggests that bankers were extremely narrow in their consideration of creditworthiness, focusing on domestic political and economic factors to the exclusion of the international environment that shaped lending patterns. Yet it has primarily been shifts in the international economy transmitted to the developing countries that has precipitated the debt crisis. The analysis also supports the thesis put forward by Kindleberger, [5] that international bank lending follows a boom- bust cycle that has occurred numerous times throughout history. The implications of these conclusions for the current debt situation are discussed in chapter five.

FIGURE ONE

TOTAL PRIVATE DEBT OF DEVELOPING COUNTRIES

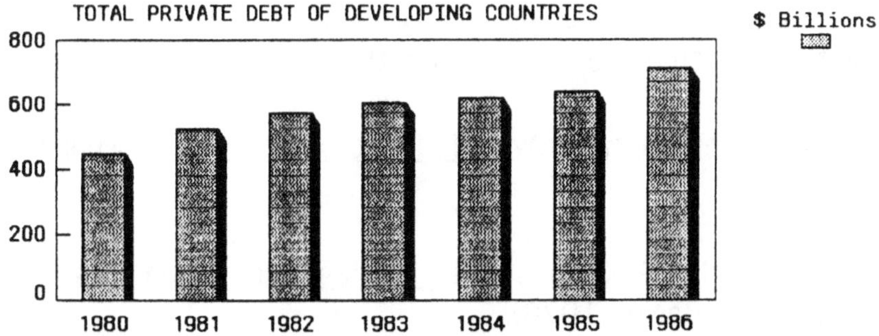

Source: World Bank, Development and Debt Service, 1986, p.xi

I: REFERENCES

[1] See, for example, Harold Lever and Christopher Huhne, Debt and Danger: The World Financial Crisis, for an good summary of the origins of the crisis and interesting policy prescriptions; William Cline, International Debt: Systemic Risk and Policy Response, for a thorough treatment of bank vulnerability; and Gordon Smith and John Cuddington ed., International Debt and the Developing Countries for good case studies of Mexico and Korea; also see bibliography.

[2] These figures include both short term debt-estimated for the first time by the World Bank and long term debt from private sources. Most estimates of LDC debt do not include short term debt. See Development and Debt Service, p. xi.

[3] This is not to argue that the debt problem of the poorer developing countries, particularly the African countries is inconsequential, only that the largest amount of debt is owed by the wealthier developing countries.

[4] See Morgan Guaranty World Financial Markets, February, 1986, p. 3.

[5] See Charles P. Kindleberger, Manias, Panics and Crises, (New York: Basic Books, 1978).

II: THE SETTING

The decade of the 1970's was a time of turbulence and change in the world economy. The increased cost of oil dramatically affected the domestic economies and politics of both the industrialized and the developing countries. As the decade of the 1980's began, recession and high interest rates in the industrialized world, combined with worsening terms of trade in the developing countries led to the debt shocks of 1982.

The international capital markets were the vehicle for much of the change and reorganization of capital flows which occurred during this period. For the developing countries, loans from private, commercial banks became an important source of external capital used to finance both oil imports and general development plans. According to the World Bank, private commercial bank lending was the component of external finance that grew most rapidly from 1970 to 1980.[1] Private commercial bank lending was estimated at $32 billion in 1970. By 1980, counting both short and long term debt, that figure had reached $448 billion. Current estimates for 1987 put both short and long term debt to private banks at more than $700 billion[2]. The U.S. banks have been important players in the debt game. The U.S. banks exposure (total claims) to all the developing countries reached a peak in 1984 of $107.8 billion, (See Figure One). Since that time new capital from the private banks to the developing countries has dropped off dramatically

Two key developments in international capital markets facilitated this massive transfer of capital from the private banks to the developing countries: the rise of the Eurocurrency market and the concurrent use of syndicated loans

The term Eurocurrency is something of a misnomer. The Eurocurrency market transcends the boundaries of Europe proper and is now worldwide in scope. This stateless market arose in response to the growing importance of international trade and investment, particularly that dominated in dollars, and as a response to several capital control measures in the U.S., specifically the Voluntary Restraint Program of 1965 and the Foreign Direct Investment Act of 1968. These restrictive programs which were designed to stem the outflow of U.S. dollars, actually stimulated the growth of the Eurocurrency market. The Eurocurrency market registered a phenomenal growth in the 1970's. According to the Bank for International Settlement (BIS) deposits in this market rose dramatically from $55 billion in 1965 to $650 billion in 1975 and to $2100 by the end of 1984. Eurocurrency loans to the non-OPEC LDC's were an important part of this growth. These loans grew from twenty-two percent of the total loaned in 1972 to forty-three percent in 1979.[3]

The second important development which contributed to the increase in loans to the LDC borrowers was syndication. The volume of syndicated loans paralleled the growth of the Eurocurrency market (where most of these loans were generated). In 1972, (the first year of reliable statistics), $11.4 billion was raised in syndicated loans. By 1981, volume had reached a staggering $178 billion, which was a total "greater than the GNP of all but the world's fourteen largest countries."[4] (See Figure Two).

FIGURE ONE

EXPOSURE OF U.S. BANKS TO THE DEVELOPING COUNTRIES

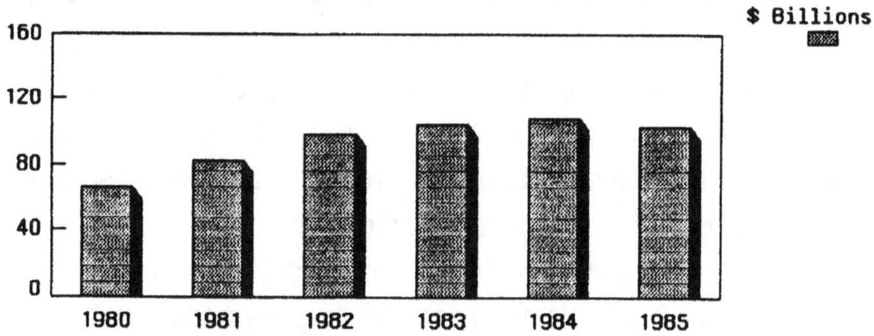

Source: World Bank, Development and Debt Service, 1986, p. xx.

FIGURE TWO

VOLUME OF SYNDICATED LOANS IN THE EUROCURRENCY MARKET

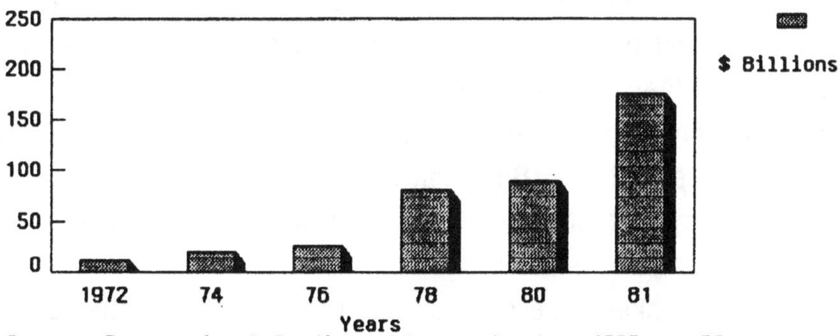

Source: International Syndicated Loans, London, 1983, p. 56.

These syndicated loans were used most frequently by international banks in their dealings with the developing countries in the 1970's, according to the Organization of Economic Cooperation and Development (OECD). According to this group, "medium and long-term syndicated international bank lending constituted the most important source of borrowed funds for the developing countries." [5]

In a syndicated loan, the loan is shared by a number of banks and the risk of default is spread among the banks. While many banks share a syndicated loan, only one lead bank exists for each loan. The lead bank prepares a placement memorandum for all lenders in the transaction which describes the transaction and provides information about the borrower. [6] While the participating banks are supposed to prepare their own analysis of the borrower, in practice, the lead banks' analysis shapes that of the other banks in the syndication. As one expert admitted, "by the rest of the syndicate, the managing leader is presumed to enjoy the most intimate knowledge of the borrower and therefore is in a favored position to develop its own appraisal as well as to provide relatively complete information, permitting other syndicate member to make their own assessment." [7] Bankers within the lead bank have the critical responsibility for information gathering and dissemination.

The lead bankers' perception of the creditworthiness of a potential borrower greatly influences the perception of risk for other participants in a syndicated loan. While many banks are involved in a syndicated loan, the analyses prepared by the lead bank regarding the borrowers' creditworthiness plays a critical role in shaping the decision to lend for the other participants.

The research presented below analyzed the behavior of six banks when one of these banks was the lead bank in a syndicated Eurocurrency loan to a developing country. Six banks and two distinct lending periods were examined. The banks: Citicorp, Bank of America, Chase Manhattan, Bankers Trust, Morgan Guaranty and Manufacturers Hanover were deeply involved in lending to the developing countries in the early 1970's. As a group, their earnings from foreign business increased from 18.5 percent (median) in 1970 to 60 percent by 1976 [8]. During the heydays of the early 1970's these banks were considered to be leaders in the area of country risk analysis by other banks in the United States. In addition, these banks were willing either to allow senior executives to be interviewed on the topic of country risk and creditworthiness and/or made available copies of internal documents on these topics. [9]

Two periods of lending were examined: 1972 through mid-1974 and mid-1977 through mid-1980. These two time periods differed in important ways. The first period of lending was a borrowers market. According to the Federal reserve, "by mid-1972, lenders had developed confidence in the market, credit volumes rose, spreads began to narrow and maturities lengthened." [10] By mid-1974, however, this situation had changed. With the failure of the Bankhaus Herstatt and the Franklin National Bank, the market shifted rapidly towards a lenders market, with a significant tightening of credit terms. Bankers became more concerned about their exposure to the developing countries. The lenders market lasted throughout most of the rest of the decade.

Research was conducted in several stages during a period from 1979-81. Initially interviews were conducted, to the extent possible, with executives who had been involved in the decision-making on LDC loans during the first period of lending examined. Where these individuals were unavailable, all relevant documents were studied. A second round of interviews was conducted during 1980 and 1981 with bankers who had major responsibilities for loans to developing countries during the second period of lending. The purpose of these interviews was to pin down what factors bankers' examined when assessing LDC creditworthiness.

Based on the interviews and written documents made available by the banks it became evident that the six banks were not homogeneous in their image of LDC creditworthiness during the first period of lending examined: 1972 through mid-1974 . During this first lending period, the six banks appeared to have two different images or mental sets regarding creditworthiness: one that was conservative in its outlook and another that was more aggressive. (See Table One). The conservative bankers indicated that while they were not risk takers, they nevertheless did lend to LDC governments which met specific criteria set forth by these bankers, and for specific purposes. Their image of what constituted a creditworthy status differed from the aggressive bankers who, for example, were less concerned with political risk than were the conservative bankers. During the second period of lending the six banks shared a common image of creditworthiness,

Table One

1972 Through Mid 1974

The Conservative Image

Chase Manhattan
Morgan Guaranty
Manufacturers Hanover

The Aggressive Image

Citibank
Bankers Trust
Bank of America

The Merged Image

Mid-1977 Through Mid-1980

Chase Manhattan
Morgan Guaranty
Manufacturers Hanover
Citibank

what has been termed a merged image. Three models representing the different images of creditworthiness were constructed. Two models were built for the first period of lending when there were separate views or images of creditworthiness by the bankers; and a single model was built for the second period of lending. The results of the models or simulations were compared to empirical data to see if there was a correspondence between the bankers' images of LDC creditworthiness and their behavior regarding loans during the two time periods. The methodology used in representing the bankers' knowledge is presented in the next chapter and a more thorough discussion of the methodology and simulator is covered in Appendix One. The results of the simulations, the images, are then compared to the data on loans and country characteristics. These images or models are evaluated and the implications of the models are discussed in chapters four and five.

II: REFERENCES

[1] World Bank, World Development Report, 1981. (New York: Oxford University Press, 1981): p. 52.

[2] See World Bank, Development and Debt Service: Dilemma of the 1980's. (Washington, D.C., :The World Bank, 1986): p. xi

[3] Organization for Economic Cooperation and Development, Development Cooperation, 1979. (Paris: OECD, 1979): p. 66 and Organization for Economic Cooperation and Development, The Internationalization of Banking: The Policy Issues. (Paris: OECD, 1983).

[4] Robert P. McDonald, International Syndicated Loans. (London: Euromoney Publications): p. 1. This book gives a thorough overview of the syndication process.

[5] Organization for Economic Cooperation and Development, Development Cooperation, 1979. (Paris:OECD, 1979): p. 94.

[6] S.M. Yassukovich, "The Duties of a Lead Manager." Euromoney (August 1974): p. 6.

[7] Ibid., p. 4.
Also see Robert P. McDonald, International Syndicated Loans, Section II.

[8] See United Nations, Transnational Corporations in World

Development, (New York, 1978), p. 218.

[9] All those interviewed were guaranteed anonymity.

[9] Federal Reserve Bank of New York. "The Pricing of Syndicated Eurocurrency Credits." Quarterly Review. Vol. 5 No. 2 (Summer 1980): p. 44.

III: METHODOLOGY

The knowledge gained from interviews and documents was the basis for the development of the bankers' decision rules or algorithms regarding creditworthiness. These decision rules were then incorporated into artificial-intelligence based simulations or models. The methodology underlying these models is discussed below, (and in appendix one). The models were then compared to empirical data on loans, spreads and country characteristics. These results are presented in the next chapter.

The simulation models have their roots in artificial intelligence. The central goal of the field of artificial intelligence is to understand, explain and represent human intelligence with the aid of computers.

Artificial intelligence (AI) is a broad field of study crossing several disciplines including: computer science, cognitive science, linguistics and philosophy. [1] In the past several decades, a great deal of cross fertilization has occurred among these fields, and as result, researchers in artificial intelligence and cognitive science have made significant strides in understanding and modeling human intelligence.

There are two key concepts inherent in this definition of artificial intelligence: intelligence and representation. Attempts at defining both of these concepts have led to major debates within the field.

One group of scholars, representing what has been called the "strong" view of AI, equates cognition with computation. As Zenon Pylyshyn, perhaps the most eloquent representative of this group has stated:

> "One of the central proposals that I examine is the thesis that what makes it possible for humans to act on the basis of representations is that they instantiate such representations physically as cognitive codes and that their behavior is a causal consequence of operations carried out on these codes. Since this is precisely what computers do, my proposal amounts to a claim that cognition *is* a type of computation." [2]

Proponents of the "weak" view of AI see their computer programs as representations of various theoretical propositions about human cognition, perception, movement and behavior, but they do no necessarily equate the workings of the mind with that of a computer.

While this debate rages on, several major contributions have emerged from both AI and cognitive science which raise important questions for the social sciences. None of the areas addressed by these two fields is more important than the questioning of the traditional concept of rationality as it applies to human behavior and decision-making.

Traditional conceptions of rationality have emphasized search for choices among a set of alternatives. The prerequisites for this view of decision-making include, complete information about all alternatives along with the consequences of a choice and the ability to rank order preferences. The view of decision-making has come under attack by many recently, including Herbert Simon, who developed the notion of bounded rationality. According to Simon:

> It is obviously impossible for the individual to know 'all' his alternatives or 'all' of their consequences, and this impossibility is an important departure of actual behavior from the model of objective rationality. [3]

Recent work by Johnson-Laird in philosophy and research by Tversky and Kahneman, and Kahneman, Slovic and Tversky in cognitive science, also cast serious doubts on traditional assumptions of rationality.

These researchers have pointed out the importance of mental models which mediate between thought and choice, and the importance of the way in which a problem or decision is "framed" or the manner in which the context of decision-making shapes the decision. Instead of rationally based behavior, recent research suggests that decision making is rule based, that humans use heuristics or rules of thumb, in interpreting situations and making choices.

Recent work in political science suggests that these heuristics are often based on precedent and analogy. As Majeski stated:

> Policymakers do not maximize. They do not evaluate all alternatives or calculate expected

> utilities. They do not use rigid unchanging organizational standard operating procedures. In order to deal with complex problems, policymakers learn from experience, remember, and package their knowledge in the form of heuristics and decision rules. These rules are verbal. Policymakers take verbal knowledge (memory, current information, goals, ideological beliefs) and use verbal rules to generate behavior, (decision, recommendations and the like). [4]

If one accepts the view that behavior is rule following and that these rules are accessible, that our images of the world shape our thoughts and decisions, that the manner in which a problem or idea is framed shapes our choices, how then can this type of knowledge be represented? The field of AI offers several appropriate techniques useful in representing symbolic knowledge including production systems, frames, scripts and most recently, object oriented representation.

The most common type of knowledge representation is called a production or rule based system. Rule based systems contain a knowledge base and an inference mechanism which operates on the rules. The rules contain two components: if and then clauses. The left side of the rule states that if certain conditions exist, then certain actions are to take place.

Rule based systems have become one of the most widely used AI applications, particularly in the building of expert systems. Expert systems mimic the expertise of an individual in a specific domain and are oriented toward problem-solving.

Expert systems have become popular in domains where knowledge is fairly complete and uncontroversial. An expert system then is a knowledge base containing both symbolic information and an inference engine that is meant to mimic the knowledge of an expert in a limited, well-understood field. Examples of such systems are MYCIN, a medical diagnostic program, DENDRAL, used by chemists, and PROSPECTOR, used by geologists to uncover mineral deposits.

Many expert systems have been developed recently in fields ranging from defense to banking and finance, and a rule based system has been developed in the field of international relations to represent the interaction between China and India.[5] More recently, the object oriented paradigm and languages have become important and useful to researchers in AI and cognitive science.[6] Object orientation allows the developer of a program to think in terms natural to the domain being represented. Both abstract and concrete concepts ranging from ideas to physical objects are represented as objects. A one-to-one correspondence between the "real world" and the model is thereby created.

These developments and discoveries have led to increased knowledge about language comprehension and processing, human understanding of vision and movement, and of cognitive processes in general. Two aspects of AI and cognitive science, the notions and systems of knowledge representation, and the focus on decision making and rationality by researchers in cognitive science science, have attracted the attention of political scientists.

Political scientists have begun to adopt several of the notions developed ion the fields of AI and cognitive science particularly the idea that human behavior follows discoverable rules and that knowledge about the rules of human thought and behavior can be represented symbolically.

Most of the work in political science and international relations that has drawn on the tools and techniques of artificial intelligence and the assumptions of cognitive science have been in the areas of foreign policy and national security studies. Thorson and Sylvan, for example, have pioneered the notion of intentional inferencing. According to Thorson, a system is considered intentional if "that system's behavior can frequently be understood by predicting a collection of beliefs, desires, hopes, goals policies, and so on to that system." [7] These authors have incorporated their ideas about intentional inferencing into a system that attempts to explain President Kennedy's decision-making processes during the Cuban missile crisis. They tested the validity of their model by examining how the model handles counterfactuals. That is they ran their model with modified version of what actually happened during the Cuban missile crisis to determine whether the model acted in a plausible manner-in the way President Kennedy would have behaved if faced with similar situations. [8]

Majeski has constructed a "recommendation model for war involvement." He examined four stages of the Vietnam War and one stage of the Korean War to test his notions of the plausibility and generalizability of general cultural rules in shaping recommendations during a war period.

Valerie Hudson has developed a rule based production system which represents the border confrontation between China and India in 1962. Both the Hudson and Majeski models developed the rules and heuristics contained in their systems by interpreting primary and historical documents rather than building actor specific rules.

Tanaka, in building the China_Watcher system incorporated both the perceptions of China's leaders in interpreting the external world and Tanaka's interpretations of China's external behavior.

Other interesting examples of AI based models in political science and international relations include Phillips' simulations of the Middle East, Schrodt's work on pattern matching and set prediction and Davis' studies on deterrence.[9]

The models presented below differ from much of the current work in AI and political science in a number of important respects. The AI models are quite primitive, developed as they were when the field of knowledge representation within computer science was in its infancy. Secondly, they are actor specific models. They are meant to represent only the specific bankers interviewed. As such, the models cannot be generalized to all U.S. bankers, or all international bankers. They are meant only to represent the six major bankers and banks involved in lending from 1972 through 1980. This does not mean, however, that these models cannot give us useful information about how these banks and bankers viewed the international lending situation, particularly the creditworthiness criteria for the developing country borrowers, and what the implications may be, of these mental models.

These models then can be considered as very primitive expert systems which represent the belief systems of the six bankers discussed in chapter two. (A further discussion of the methodology is presented in appendix one.)

The models were built after interviewing the "experts" in international lending at the six U.S. banks under consideration during the two time periods. These models are compared to data on loans by their banks, to see if the models are accurate representations of the bankers' beliefs regarding creditworthiness, to see if there is a correspondence between their belief systems and their behavior.

The simulation models that were built to represent bankers' beliefs regarding creditworthiness are based on the expert knowledge of the bankers who were interviewed and of that contained in the documents that were reviewed. The bankers' subjective perceptions or expert opinion regarding creditworthiness, the set of conditions deemed essential for loans to be made, were represented using conditional statements or algorithms. The results of the simulations, which are also algorithms, are discussed in chapter four.

The algorithms or chunks of informations are related via a set of links and a spontaneous computation system. The spontaneous computation, (SC), scans the entire data base, which is composed of symbolic statements linked to each other in different ways, [10] to see which statements should be triggered. In other words, the SC "causes computations to be invoked or aborted not because some other part of the model has requested so but because a computations 'trigger pattern' has matched some condition in the system." [11] The simulator actually consists of three parts: the initial representation of chunks of informations or algorithms via linked events; a spontaneous computation model of each link in the initial representation; and the running of the model which involves setting down the initial conditions (IC) and trigger. Both the initial condition and the trigger can be changed from one run to the next.

This type of model allows one to replicate different situations by altering the 'initial conditions' that set the model running, for example, altering the initial conditions to represent a borrowers or a lenders market. They also allow a researcher to ask 'what if' types of questions, thus generating both explanations of past decisions and if the models match the behavior, prediction. As one researcher has stated, "the customary distinctions between different kinds of analytic products are blurred in research in the artificial intelligence tradition. Generative explanations are often sought in artificial intelligence research. This means that an artificial-intelligence based computer program often attempts to produce or generate a particular class of outcomes...the model can be used to generate either explanation or prediction depending on whether the analyst in using the model as a representation of the past or of the future." [12]

The bankers' expert knowledge regarding LDC creditworthiness was represented in several models, two for the first period of lending, (conservative and aggressive image), and one for the second period (merged image). If the models are accurate representations, then there should be a strong relationship between these models or images and the bankers' behavior towards lending to the developing countries. Specifically the countries which better fit the image should have received more from the bankers and on better terms.

The images or decision rules generated by the simulations represent in a sense, a set of independent variables which should explain bankers' behavior on lending policies towards LDC governments, the dependent variables. The results of the simulations were compared to empirical data on loan volume, spreads and country characteristics to see if the bankers' images matched their behavior on lending.

The data on loan volume and spreads come from the World Bank's Capital Markets System. The volume was calculated by simply adding up the total amounts of loans to specific developing country borrowers for the different time periods examined. The calculation of the model spread involved five steps (See Formula 3.1). The calculation of the modal spread involved five steps. [12]

The total amount of all loans for individual country ij, was calculated. Then, the different spreads, s for individual countries for the time period considered, were identified. The sum of loans for individual country j, at spread si,j was then computed. Next, the percentage of loans for for country j, at spread si,j was calculated. Finally, the modal spread for each individual country was chosen to represent the most frequent spread for country j at each time period. The formula allows for the computation of the the volume and terms of loans received by individual countries.

FORMULA 3.1

Calculation of modal spread for individual country j.

$$S_j = (s_{1,j}, s_{2,j}, \ldots s_{n_j,j}) = \text{all spreads for country } j.$$

$$T_j\,(s_{i,j}) = \text{the sum of all loans for country } j \text{ at spread } s_{i,j}.$$

$$U_j = \sum_{i=1}^{n_j} U_j\,(s_{i,j}) = \text{total loans for country } j.$$

$$P_{i,j} = \frac{T_j\,(s_{i,j})}{U_j} \times 100 = \text{the percentage of loans for country } j \text{ at spread } s_{i,j}.$$

The most frequent spread for each country, the modal spread, was then chosen and used to rank countries according to modal spreads from best spreads to worst spreads received.

The data on loans represent loans from the six banks when one of the banks was the lead bank in a syndicated Eurocurrency loan to a LDC government. For the first period of lending from 1972 through mid-1974 the data were separated into two sets. When either Chase Manhattan, Morgan Guaranty or Manufacturers Hanover was the lead bank, the data was used to test the conservative image. For the aggressive image, the data on loans represent loans when Citibank, Bankers Trust or Bank of America was the lead bank during the same period. The data on loans for the second period of lending, from mid-1977 through mid-1980, represent loans when any one of the six banks was the lead bank in a syndicated loan to an LDC government. These data represent in a sense, dependent variables. The algorithms are then compared to the countries which received loans from the banks to see if there is a match between the algorithms and the loans (i.e. the images and the behavior of the bankers). The data on country characteristics represent to the extent possible, data examined by bankers before and during the decision period.

III: REFERENCES

[1] For excellent introductions to the field see: Avron Barr and Edward Feigenbaum, The Handbook of Artificial Intelligence, Volumes
1-3. (Los Altos, California: William Kaufmann Inc., 1981.), and Howard Gardner, Minds New Science: The Cognitive Revolution in the Computer Age, (New York: Basic Books, 1985).

[2] Zenon Pylyshyn, Computation and Cognition: Toward A Foundation for Cognitive Science, (Cambridge, Massachusetts: MIT Press, 1984.): xiii.

[3] Herbert Simon, Administrative Behavior 3rd Edition. (New York: The Free Press, 1976): p. 67.

[4] Stephen Majeski, " A Recommendation Model of War Initiation: Plausibility and Generalizability of General Cultural Rules," In Artificial Intelligence and National Security, edited by Stephen Cimbala (Lexington, Massachusetts: Lexington Books.): p. 62-63.

[5] For a general discussion of expert systems see Deborah Wolfgram, Expert Systems for the Technical Professional (New York: John Wiley and Sons, 1987); and for examples of expert systems in international relations and political science see

---

Stephen Cimbala ed., Artificial Intelligence and National Security, (Lexington, Massachusetts: Lexington Books, 1987).

[6] See Adele Goldberg, Smalltalk-80 The Interactive Programming Environment (Reading, Massachusetts: Addison-Wesley Publishing 1984

[7] Stuart Thorson, ""Intentional Inferencing in Foreign Policy: An AI Approach." In Foreign Policy Decision Making, edited by Donald Sylvan and Steve Chan, (New York: Praeger Publishers, 1984): 280.

[8] See Stuart Thorson and Donald Sylvan, "Counterfactuals and the Cuban missile Crisis," International Studies Quarterly 26 (December 1982): pp. 539-71.

[9] See articles by these authors in, Cimbala, 1987. See also edited volume by Sylvan and Chan, 1984.

[10] Appendix one contains a thorough discussion of the manner in which symbolic statements can be related or linked.

[11] Chuck Rieger, "The Causal Representation and Simulation of Physical Mechanisms." University of Maryland, TR-495 (1976): p. 1.

[12] Steve Chan and Donald Sylvan, "Foreign Policy Decision Making: An Overview." In Foreign Policy Decision Making, edited by Donald Sylvan and Steve Chan (New York: Praeger, 1984): p. 9. Also see: Roger Schank and Robert Abelson, Scripts, Plans, Goals and Understanding: An Inquiry into Human Knowledge

---

Structures. (Hillsdale, New Jersey: Erlbaum Publications, 1977)., and Roger Schank and Kenneth Colby, eds., Computer Models of Thought and Language. (San Francisco: Freeman, 1973).

[12] The spreads were used as an indicator of risk, instead of other indicators such as maturities, because at the time the study was conducted, the maturities of loans were not available for all loans examined.

IV: IMAGES AND BEHAVIOR

This chapter examines how six international bankers assessed the creditworthiness of the developing country borrowers and what the relationship was between their images of creditworthiness and their lending behavior. For each lending period considered, the implications of this relationship for the developing country borrowers is assessed.

The image of creditworthiness for the conservative bankers during the first period of lending is presented and compared to empirical data on loans, followed by that for the aggressive bankers. Finally the merged image of creditworthiness for the second period of lending is presented and analyzed.

During the initial period of lending, the conservative bankers lent to twelve developing countries. The total amount loaned was $1580.9 million, (See Table 4.1. All tables are located at the end of the chapter.)

These bankers, when compared to the aggressive bankers on amount loaned, were risk averters. They lent 35.1 percent less than the aggressive bankers. This is also reflected in the relationship between the amount loaned and the spread. The amount loaned and the spread should coincide if both indicators are measuring a common representation of risk. For the conservative bankers, the opposite held during this initial period of lending. The countries which received the most from these bankers, in general did not receive the best terms. There was a negative, but weak, relationship between the amount loaned and the spread (r^2=-.184). The countries which borrowed the most from these bankers did not receive the best terms as represented by the spreads. This is an indication that the bankers protected themselves during this initial period of lending, even though it was a borrower's market. Since the total amount loaned is a clearer indicator of risk assessment, the total amount loaned or volume was used as the indicator of creditworthiness and compared to the country characteristics generated by the simulation of the conservative bankers' image of creditworthiness.

When the simulation of the conservative image was run reflecting the market conditions of the first period of lending, ten algorithms were triggered. Each statement that was triggered in the simulation was compared to empirical data to determine whether there was a relationship between the image and the behavior on lending. The volume of lending was used to rank the countries, and a rank order correlation coefficient was computed for the independent variables represented by the algorithms, where the two variables were at least ordinal level variables, and pearson's r (correlation coefficient) was computed when the variables reached the interval level.

Did the conservative bankers lend to countries which reflected the algorithms generated by the simulation? Can the image of creditworthiness explain the behavior of the conservative bankers towards lending to LDC governments? The foremost concern of the conservative bankers was with the stability of the LDC government. They measured this not only by considering information on elections or transfers of power but also on recent terrorist activity within the country. According to these bankers, terrorism was a strong indicator of a government's stability. The rank order correlation between volume loaned and data on terrorist activity for the countries which received loans from these banks, (r_s=.384), indicates that the countries which received the most from these bankers also had the smallest amount of terrorist activity during the initial period of lending, (See Table 4.2).

For the conservative bankers, another indicator of government stability was the manner in which governmental power was transferred. A stable government, according to this image, changed power in an orderly, non-violent fashion. In general, all of the countries, except Peru, which received loans from the conservative bankers matched this image of a stable and orderly transfer of power (See Table 4.3). Governments which received loans from these bankers were stable (as defined by the bankers) and those who received the greatest amount experienced the smallest amount of terrorist activity within the country.

An additional criterion for the conservative bankers was a governments' attitude toward foreign direct investment.

This was important, according to the bankers, because many of their clients had existing operations within many of the developing countries. The conservative bankers examined in particular the governments' attitude towards U.S. based firms.

The six countries which received the largest amount in loans from these banks had the highest percentage of direct investment (of all LDC's which allowed foreign investment), and all of these countries except for Brazil and Peru, encouraged U.S. direct investment, (See Tables 4.4 to 4.6). With only two exceptions, during the period preceding the initial period of lending, all of the countries which received loans from the conservative bankers either allowed or actively encouraged foreign direct investment from the U.S. These same countries were also considered safe for the operations of the multinational banks. Only one country imposed any restrictions on the activities of the multinational banks within their borders. Mexico barred the multinational banks from operating in the rural banking sector. In general then, there was a match between the algorithms generated by the conservative image and the indicators of political stability.

The economic analysis conducted by the conservative bankers focused on the level of development of the economy and potential growth possibilities. These bankers indicated that they would not loan to countries with G.N.P. per capita of less than $250.00 nor would they lend to countries with growth rates of less than 2.5 percent.

The first indicator on G.N.P. per capita does not entirely match the image of the conservative bankers. (See Table 4.7.) Five of the twelve countries which received loans from the conservative bankers had G.N.P.'s per capita of less than $250.00. On the other hand, these same countries had high rates of growth during this same period. All twelve countries had growth rates above 2.5 percent for the period 1960-1968 preceding the initial lending period. The rank order correlation between amount loaned and G.N.P per capita is positive, but very weak (r_s=.070) while the correlation between amount and growth rate is stronger, and also positive (r_s= .273). Those countries which received the greatest amount from these bankers, in general also had the strongest economies on these measures.

An additional factor incorporated into the analysis on creditworthiness by the conservative bankers was whether the developing country had a stable and diversified source of foreign exchange. On this indicator, the bankers' image did not correspond with their lending behavior (See Table 4.8). The conservative bankers lent the most to countries which had a highly concentrated source of foreign exchange. Only two of the eight countries for which data were available in the period preceding the initial period of lending had a diversified source of foreign exchange. For Iran, the country which received the most in loans from these particular bankers, crude petroleum made up 78 percent of its foreign exchange earnings and for Brazil, which ranked third in total amount received, 44 percent of its foreign exchange earnings came from coffee, a commodity which was highly unstable during the late 1960's and early 1970's.

This mismatch between the bankers' image of what constituted creditworthiness and their behavior on loans is significant.

These two countries ran into severe difficulties with the banks later in the 1970's. However, both of these countries also scored higher on the political indicators deemed important by the conservative bankers, perhaps overriding the low ranking on this issue.

On an additional indicator, the bankers' behavior did not coincide closely with their images. The conservative bankers' image indicated that the structure of long term debt preceding the initial period of lending, should have consisted primarily of bilateral (government to government) debt. For none of the countries which received loans from the conservative bankers, was their debt primarily bilateral in nature. For all of these countries, the structure of their debt in 1970 consisted mainly of suppliers credits, or for some of the major borrowers, it already consisted of debt to private sources. [1]

Finally, the conservative bankers image indicated that a commitment to human development, particularly to education, on the part of the LDC government was a factor although a secondary one, in the assessment of creditworthiness. While it was difficult to pinpoint the manner in which bankers defined this concept, one indicator frequently mentioned was the literacy rate. For all of the countries which received loans form the conservative bankers, there was a positive, but weak, relationship (r_s= .272) between the ranking on literacy and the ranking on amount received from the conservative bankers. (See Table 4.9).

Except for the indicators on degree of concentration of exports and that for the structure of debt, the bankers' image of creditworthiness generated by the simulation, in general explained the lending behavior of these bankers. Most importantly from their perspective, they lent to countries considered politically stable, open to foreign direct investment and countries which compared to other developing countries, had strong economies. Where their behavior did not match their image, (particularly with Iran, Peru and Brazil), debt service problems arose fairly soon after the initial period of lending. The implications for the developing countries were quite clear.

Only countries which were considered politically stable, countries which were open to the international economy and those which had already reached a fairly high level of growth received loans from these bankers.

The aggressive bankers' image of creditworthiness differed significantly from that of the conservative bankers. Their behavior on lending also differed dramatically.

The aggressive bankers lent almost a billion dollars more during the same initial period of lending, compared to the conservative bankers. They also lent to almost twice the number of developing countries than the conservative bankers. (See Table 4.10). Only twelve developing countries received loans from the conservative bankers, totalling $1580.9 million, compared to twenty-two developing countries, receiving $2433.6 million from the aggressive bankers. The aggressive bankers, like the conservative bankers, did not give the best terms to countries which borrowed the most from them. The negative relationship between amount loaned and modal spread was stronger for this set of bankers than it was for the conservative bankers (r^2= -.247). Again, this is a surprising finding in that this relationship occurred in a borrowers market.

The algorithms generated by the simulation for the aggressive bankers differed from those representing the conservative bankers. The image generated for the aggressive bankers reflected an almost exclusive concern with the performance of the economy on the growth of exports. As risk takers, these bankers were interested primarily in whether there was a visible and growing source of foreign exchange.

The aggressive bankers' image focused on the outward thrust of the economy. They were interested primarily in indicators which reflected this image. Compared to the conservative bankers, they were much less concerned with political risk. For these bankers, an ability to repay was reflected in the growth of exports, and the willingness to repay was not in doubt. In fact, according to the image generated by these bankers, if there had not been any rescheduling of public debt nor had their been a violent overthrow of the government in five years preceding lending, then domestic politics was unimportant in making the decision to lend.

A primary indicator for the aggressive bankers was the major type of export commodity for the country under consideration for a loan. Countries whose major export commodity was either a natural resource (particularly oil) or an agricultural product whose prices were either stable or growing for the period preceding lending, were strong candidates for lending. Except for Korea, the major export in the period preceding the initial period of lending for all of the countries which received loans from the aggressive bankers, was either a natural resource or an agricultural product. (See Table 4.11). In addition, for all but five of the nineteen countries for which data were available, the growth rate of these exports was greater than five percent during the period from 1960 through 1968. (See Table (4.12).

The image generated for the aggressive bankers indicated that these bankers would not lend to countries whose debt-service to exports ratio was greater than fifteen percent. All but four of the countries (Argentina, Mexico, Korea and Taiwan) which received loans from the aggressive bankers matched the image on this indicator. (See Table 4.13). There is a fairly strong, positive relationship between the ranking on amount loaned by the aggressive bankers and the ranking (from lowest to highest) on the debt-service ratio (r_s= .335). This means that the countries which received the greatest amount also had the lowest debt-service ratio.

The only political factor generated by the aggressive image related to rescheduling. The aggressive bankers indicated that they would not lend to countries which had rescheduled during five years previous to lending. Two countries which did receive loans from these bankers had rescheduled during the five years prior to the loan period (Peru and Indonesia) and one country, Turkey, had rescheduled six years prior to the initial period of lending. (See Table 4.14).

As with the conservative bankers, when there was a mismatch between the aggressive image and lending behavior, often debt-service difficulties arose. All three of the countries which had rescheduled before the onset of lending, have experienced difficulties with debt servicing.

All of the countries which did receive loans form the aggressive bankers matched the image of political stability indicated by the aggressive image. None of the countries had experienced a violent overthrow in the five years preceding the loan period, and only one country experienced a measurable amount of animosity towards foreign direct investment during this same period. That country, Jamaica, experienced a major shift in its attitude towards foreign direct investment from 1972 to 1980. Jamaica, like Turkey, Peru and Indonesia, countries which did not match the aggressive bankers image of creditworthiness on major issues, were later forced to reschedule their debt with these banks.

Both the conservative and the aggressive images and behavior had important implications for the developing countries. The conservative image emphasized political stability. A borrower had to be in control of its political system (in a manner deemed important by the bankers) before they received loans from these bankers. The aggressive bankers were more interested in the type and growth of exports in the borrower country. The majority of countries which received loans from these bankers depended on primary products as their major source of foreign exchange and most had experienced growth in their export sector in the period preceding the onset of lending. Furthermore, both images indicated that countries which were open to foreign investment were more likely to receive loans.

These two images and the behavior they explained, changed during the 1970's due to both changes in the world economy and changes in the nature of the relationship between lenders and borrowers.

During the mid-1970's the relationship between the major U.S. banks and the LDC borrowers evolved considerably. On the international scene, the U.S. banks were confronted with increased competition from the Japanese and European banks, and at home faced increase surveillance and potential regulation. Perhaps one of the most important changes resulted from increased information sharing among banks regarding potential developing country borrowers. As a result of these changes, the image of creditworthiness tended to merge for the six banks examined. A standardized, shared set of concerns emerged. Each of the algorithms generated by the merged image of creditworthiness is assessed below.

Many more countries received loans from the six banks during the second period of lending. Forty-eight countries entered into loan agreements with the six banks during the second period compared to a total of thirty four for both the aggressive and conservative banks in the first period of lending. (See Table 4.15). The relationship between the spread and the amount received during this second period differed from the relationship evident in the first period. From mid-1977 through mid-1980, there was a strong positive relationship between the amount loaned and the terms received. This means that the more a country borrowed from these banks, the better spreads it received. This is an important reversal of the relationship which existed from mid-1972 through 1974. It signifies that some of the borrowers developed bargaining power with the banks (and it signifies increased competition for loans) and that they were able to secure better terms on loans compared to the earlier period of lending.

A fundamental change in the bankers' image occurred in regard to the purpose of the loans. During the first lending period, the bankers' image indicated that general purpose loans for general development or balance of payments purposes were acceptable. During the second period of lending, the merged image indicated that lending was likely for projects, rather than general balance of payment support. Projects which related to the development of energy resources and natural resource exploration and development were favored. This algorithm is apparently confirmed when one examines data on the purpose of loans during the second period of lending. According to data from the World Bank's Capital Markets System data base, the purpose of 50.1 percent of the loans during this second period related to the development of energy projects or natural resource exploration and development while only 4 percent of the loans were for general purposes. While the trend during this second period of lending seemed to be in the direction of funding for natural resource development, and confirms the merged image, this data must be regarded with caution. The tracking of loans from the private banks once the loan has been dispersed, is extremely difficult. In other words, loans for specific purposes may not have been used for these purposes.

A country's relationship with the IMF was also an important determinant of creditworthiness according to the merged image.

The relationship of the LDC borrowers with the IMF also became an important factor in the deliberation on creditworthiness, particularly if the country under consideration experienced debt-service difficulties in the period prior to the loan request. While several countries which received loans from the banks during the second period of lending experienced a deterioration in their relationship with the IMF, (Turkey and Sri Lanka) only two countries severed their relationship with the IMF during this period of lending, Peru and Jamaica. The importance of this factor in determining creditworthiness by the banks, obviously became more important in the 1980's. For the developing countries, many of whom approached the banks because of the attractiveness of external capital without strings attached, the importance of being on good terms with the IMF led to serious political and economic instability in the 1980's.

All of the countries which received funding from the six banks, except for Iran, in general had positive relations with the U.S. The case of Iran obviously was, and still is, a special case from the bankers' perspective. Up until the revolution, it conformed to the image of creditworthiness reflected by the merged image. Iran experienced high growth rates, actively encouraged foreign investment, and had a stable, highly demanded export commodity and strong relation with the U.S. The bankers and many observers of developing countries, underestimated the degree of political instability within Iran.

A government's attitude toward foreign investment was also a factor in assessing creditworthiness, according to the results of the simulation of the merged image. Specifically, an examination of whether there had been a negative shift away from encouraging foreign investment was indicated. The countries which received loans during the second lending period did not experience serious shifts in behavior toward foreign investment. [2]

During the second period of lending, the bankers looked more closely at figures on domestic growth than either group had during the first lending period. During the initial period the focus, particularly for the aggressive bankers, had been on export earnings. The second period of lending, the overall management of the economy was considered to be a better indicator of risk than simply growth in exports.

A positive relationship existed between amount loaned and

growth of gross domestic product from 1970 through 1976 (r^2= .302). The larger borrowers in general had the higher rates of GDP growth than the smaller borrowers. As Table 4.16 indicates, the smaller borrowers were most frequently the lower-income LDC's. A further indicator of the ability to manage the economy was the government's control over inflation and ability to implement domestic adjustment measures, (See Table 4.17).

On control of inflation, there was a negative relationship (r_2= -.307) between amount loaned and ranking on this variable. This means that the larger borrowers, usually the middle to higher-income LDC's, did not exhibit the highest rankings on controlling inflation and on reducing public expenditures. (See Table 4.18). In fact, the poorer LDC's ranked higher on these two measures of control. On the measure reflecting reduction in public expenditures for welfare and social services, five of the top ten LDC's can be considered low-income LDC's.[3] On the inflation measure, six of the top ten borrowers fall into this category. The poorer LDC's fit the image of creditworthiness on these measures better than the larger, wealthier developing countries.

Finally, the merged image indicated that the six banks would not loan to countries which had experienced public reschedulings during the 1970's unless there had been a noteworthy change in that country's economic prospects. Only if there were new energy or natural resource discoveries or a strong commitment to restructuring the economy, would the bankers consider a loan to a country which had rescheduled. Six of the nine countries which rescheduled during the mid-1970's also received loans from the six banks (See Table 4.19). At the same time, however, two of the six countries, Indonesia and Peru had made important discoveries (oil in Indonesia and copper in Peru). Two countries which rescheduled also developed new incentives for private industry and foreign investment within the country (Turkey and Chile). The final two countries which rescheduled and received loans from the banks, India and Pakistan, were not large borrowers from the six banks.

The model country to receive a loan during the second period of lending was a country that had positive relations with the IMF, made a strong commitment to domestic adjustment, was open to private foreign investment and emphasized order over democracy.

The implications of this development model have unfolded during the 1980's. The developing country borrowers have experienced significant declines in living standards and are faced with debt burdens that threaten their internal stability and that of the world economy. Contrary to what private banker Irving Friedman stated in the mid-1970's, that "for developing countries that are creditworthy for private bank borrowing, the private bankers help create a wider variety of options than they previously had in selecting their development strategy," [4] the developing country borrowers find themselves locked in to development strategies dictated by the International Monetary Fund, and more recently, the World Bank.

The six banks analyzed in this study continued to be major lenders throughout the early 1980's. By the end of 1984, their combined exposure to the four largest developing country borrowers alone, Mexico, Brazil, Argentina and Venezuela had reached $36.8 billion. (See Figure One.) Since that period, voluntary lending by the major U.S. banks has dropped off dramatically. In fact, the combined exposure of the six banks to Mexico, Brazil Argentina and Venezuela had only increased to $37.02 billion by mid-1987.[5] Not surprisingly, this lack of new capital from the private banks has generated a crises of its own.

Numerous solutions have been proposed to deal with this massive debt. Most have been developed with the primary concern of ensuring that the developing countries have sufficient capital to repay old debts. These solutions are reviewed in the final chapter with an eye toward assessing the implications of the bankers' images presented above for the current debate.

FIGURE ONE

NET FOREIGN EXPOSURE TO FOUR BIGGEST LDC BORROWERS

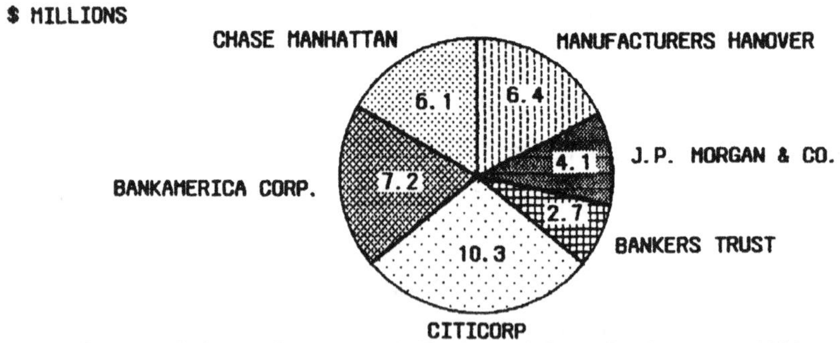

Source: Salomon Brothers, A Review of Bank Performance 1984 p. 67

TABLE 4.1

CONSERVATIVE IMAGE:
TOTAL AMOUNTS LOANED, MODAL SPREAD, PERCENTS AND RANKINGS

COUNTRY	($-MIL) AMOUNT	(1-11) RANK	MODAL SPREAD	PERCENT	(BEST-WORST 1-8) RANK BY SPREAD
IRAN	417.0	1	0.625	59.0	1
PERU	320.0	2	1.875	62.5	8
BRAZIL	191.5	3	1.000	39.1	3
ARGENTINA	156.5	4	1.750	92.0	7
PHILIPPINES	150.0	5	1.375	100.0	5
MEXICO	116.5	6	0.750	86.2	2
ECUADOR	90.0	7	1.500	100.0	5
EGYPT	80.0	8	1.000	100.0	3
COLUMBIA	80.0	8	1.375	50.0	5
KOREA	78.0	9	1.250	89.7	4
TAIWAN	30.0	10	1.500	100.0	6
NICARAGUA	6.4	11	1.500	72.7	6
TOTAL	1580.9				

Source: World Bank: Capital Markets System

TABLE 4.2

THE CONSERVATIVE IMAGE:
EMPIRICAL DATA ON TERRORIST ACTIVITY

-----Government Sanctions* Against Terrorists 1960-68-----

COUNTRY	RANK IN LOANS	RANK IN SPREADS	RANK BY SANCTIONS**	TOTAL
IRAN	1	1	4	15
PERU	2	8	3	13
BRAZIL	3	3	7	62
ARGENTINA	4	7	8	70
PHILIPPINES	5	5	2	8
MEXICO	6	2	3	13
ECUADOR	7	6	6	20
EGYPT	8	3	NA	NA
COLUMBIA	9	5	5	17
KOREA	10	4	NA	NA
TAIWAN	11	6	1	3
NICARAGUA	12	6	2	8

* A "government sanction" is defined as an action taken by the authorities neutralize, suppress or eliminate a perceived threat to the security of the government, the regime or the state.

** Only Brazil and Argentina were above the median for government sanctions for the years under study. The rankings for sanctions ranges from 1 (the lowest) to 8 (the highest).

Source: Taylor and Hudson, The World Handbook of Political and Social Indicators. (New Haven: Yale University Press, 1972).

TABLE 4.3

THE CONSERVATIVE IMAGE:
DATA ON IRREGULAR* EXECUTIVE TRANSFERS

COUNTRY	RANK ON LOANS	1965	1966	1967	1968	TOTALS***	RANK
		TRANSFERS					
IRAN	1	0	0	0	0	0	1
PERU	2	0	0	0	1	1	2
BRAZIL	3	1**	0	0	0	1	2
ARGENTINA	4	0	1	0	0	1	2
PHILIPPINES	5	NA	NA	0	0	0	1
MEXICO	6	NA	NA	0	0	0	1
ECUADOR	7	0	0	0	0	1	2
EGYPT	8	NA	NA	0	NA	0	1
COLUMBIA	9	1	0	0	0	1	2
KOREA	10	0	0	0	0	0	1
TAIWAN	11	0	0	0	0	0	1
NICARAGUA	12	0	0	0	0	0	1

* An "Irregular Executive Transfer" is a change in the office of a national executive that is accomplished outside the control of legal or customary procedures for transferring formal power in effect at the time of the event and accomplished by actual or directly threatened violence.

** Brazil's coup actually took place in 1964-1965, not just 1965 exclusively.

*** All countries were below the median ranking for each year.

Source: Taylor and Hudson, The World Handbook of Political and Social Indicators, (New Haven: Yale University Press, 1972).

TABLE 4.4

THE CONSERVATIVE IMAGE:
GOVERNMENTS' ATTITUDES TOWARDS FOREIGN DIRECT INVESTMENT, 1971

COUNTRY	RANK BY AMOUNT	RANK BY SPREAD	RANK ON TOTAL STOCK OF DIRECT INVESTMENT*	% OF TOTAL DIRECT INVESTMENT
IRAN	1	1	4	2.1
PERU	2	8	4	2.1
BRAZIL	3	3	1	11.8
ARGENTINA	4	7	3	5.1
PHILIPPINES	5	5	4	2.1
MEXICO	6	2	2	5.5
ECUADOR	7	5	NA	NA
EGYPT	8	3	NA	NA
COLUMBIA	8	5	NA	NA
KOREA	9	4	5	NA
TAIWAN	10	6	NA	NA
NICARAGUA	11	6	NA	NA

* Rank on total stock of foreign direct investment ranges from 1 (most) to 5 (least).

Source: United Nations Center on Transnational Corporations, Transnational Corporations in World Development. (New York: United Nations, 1978), p. 254.

TABLE 4.5

THE CONSERVATIVE IMAGE:
ATTITUDE TOWARD FOREIGN DIRECT INVESTMENT, 1965-1971

COUNTRY	RANK BY LOANS	ATTITUDE TOWARD FOREIGN INVESTMENT ALL	UNITED STATES
IRAN	1	Encourage*	Encourage
PERU	2	Restrictions**	Restrictions
BRAZIL	3	Restrictions	Restrictions
ARGENTINA	4	Encourage	Encourage
PHILIPPINES	5	Encourage	Encourage
MEXICO	6	Allowed***	Allowed
ECUADOR	7	Encourage	Encourage
EGYPT	8	NA	NA
COLUMBIA	9	Encourage	Encourage
KOREA	10	Encourage	Encourage
TAIWAN	11	Encourage	Encourage
NICARAGUA	12	NA	NA

* If a government encouraged foreign direct investment during this period, it meant that they allowed certain tax exemptions and made remittances on profits easy for the firms.

** If a government restricted foreign firms, it meant that foreign firms were not allowed to operate in certain sectors of the economy, or ownership was restricted.

*** If a government allowed foreign firms, it meant that they were not given any special treatment, but they were not restricted.

Sources: Information Guide to Doing Business. (New York: Price Waterhouse, 1970, 1972).
World Business Weekly, Various issues.

TABLE 4.6

THE CONSERVATIVE IMAGE:
GOVERNMENT ATTITUDE TOWARDS MULTINATIONAL BANKING

COUNTRY	RANK ON LOANS	ATTITUDE TOWARDS BANKING
IRAN	1	Encouraged*
PERU	2	Encouraged (until 1971)
BRAZIL	3	Allowed**
ARGENTINA	4	Allowed
PHILIPPINES	5	Allowed
MEXICO	6	Restrictions***
ECUADOR	7	Allowed
EGYPT	8	NA
COLUMBIA	9	Allowed
KOREA	10	NA
TAIWAN	11	Restrictions
NICARAGUA	12	NA

* If a bank was encouraged to operate in a developing country, it meant that either incentives were offered, particularly tax breaks, or in the case of Peru (until 1971) and Iran (throughout this initial period) they were explicitly protected by law.

** Allowed meant simply that. There were no special incentives, but also no restrictions.

*** A government that restricted the activity of multinational banks usually restricted them from certain sectors of the economy (often rural banking).

Sources: Information Guide to Doing Business, Price Waterhouse. Transnational Corporations in World Development, U.N.

TABLE 4.7

THE CONSERVATIVE IMAGE:
COUNTRY RANKINGS BY AMOUNT OF LOANS,
GNP PER CAPITA, AND GROWTH RATE OF GNP, 1960-68.

COUNTRY	RANK BY AMOUNT	RANK BY GNP/CAP*	GNP/CAP AMOUNT ($)	RANK BY GROWTH RATE**	GROWTH RATE AMOUNT (%)
IRAN	1	7	297	3	8.0
PERU	2	4	376	8	5.0
BRAZIL	3	5	332	7	5.1
ARGENTINA	4	1	725	12	3.2
PHILIPPINES	5	10	203	11	4.3
MEXICO	6	2	557	5	6.6
ECUADOR	7	9	259	10	4.5
EGYPT	8	12	181	6	5.7
COLUMBIA	9	8	292	9	4.8
KOREA	10	11	188	2	8.4
TAIWAN	11	6	312	1	10.0
NICARAGUA	23	3	380	4	7.6

* The GNP Per Capita ranged from $181.00 (Egypt) to $725.00 (Argentina).

** The growth rate of GNP ranged from 9.6% (Taiwan) to 3.3% (Argentina).

Source: United Nations, Review of International Trade and Development, 1970. (New York: United Nations, 1970), p. 39.

TABLE 4.8

THE CONSERVATIVE IMAGE:
DEGREE OF CONCENTRATION OF EXPORTS, 1970

COUNTRY	RANK BY LOAN	SPREAD	(% OF CONCENTRATION RANK BY DEGREE OF DIVERSIFICATION*
IRAN	1	1	8 (78%)
PERU	2	8	2 (16%)
BRAZIL	3	3	3 (44%)
ARGENTINA	4	7	NA
PHILIPPINES	5	5	1 (10%)
MEXICO	6	2	7 (71%)
ECUADOR	7	6	5 (53%)
EGYPT	8	3	4 (50%)
COLUMBIA	9	5	6 (63%)
KOREA	10	4	NA
TAIWAN	11	6	NA
NICARAGUA	12	6	NA

* The rank for degree of diversification of exports ranges from 1(Philippines 10%) to th highest degree of concentration, 8 (Iran 78%).

Source: United Nations, Review of International Trade and Development, 1970. (New York: United Nations, 1970).

TABLE 4.9

THE CONSERVATIVE IMAGE:
COMMITMENT OF GOVERNMENTS TO SERVICES FOR THE POOR, 1968

COUNTRY	RANK BY AMOUNT	SPREAD	(%) RANK BY LITERACY*	(#) RANK BY NUMBER OF PHYSICIANS/MILLION**
IRAN	1	1	10 (23%)	11 (297)
PERU	2	8	7 (61%)	4 (448)
BRAZIL	3	3	7 (61%)	8 (397)
ARGENTINA	4	7	1 (91%)	1 (1466)
PHILIPPINES	5	5	3 (72%)	2 (720)
MEXICO	6	2	5 (65%)	3 (553)
ECUADOR	7	6	5 (67%)	12 (189)
EGYPT	8	3	9 (30%)	6 (419)
COLUMBIA	9	5	5 (67%)	5 (440)
KOREA	10	4	4 (75%)	10 (351)
TAIWAN	11	6	2 (75%)	7 (413)
NICARAGUA	12	6	8 (50%)	9 (371)

* Ranking for literacy ranges from 1 (highest) to 10 (lowest).

** Ranking on physicians per million ranges from 1 (highest) to 12 (lowest).

Source: UNESCO, UNESCO Statistical Handbook, 1968. (Paris, 1968).

TABLE 4.10

THE AGGRESSIVE IMAGE: TOTAL AMOUNTS LOANED, MODAL SPREAD, PERCENTS AND RANKINGS

COUNTRY	($MIL) AMOUNT	(1-21) RANK	MODAL SPREAD	PERCENT	(BEST-WORST: 1-11) RANK BY SPREAD
BRAZIL	557.0	1	1.000	53.0	4
ARGENTINA	382.0	2	1.500	100.0	8
MEXICO	330.0	3	0.625	30.3	2
INDONESIA	187.5	4	1.500	100.0	8
PANAMA	162.0	5	1.250	70.9	6
MALAYSIA	140.0	6	1.250	100.0	5
PERU	130.0	7	1.750	100.0	10
KOREA	110.0	8	1.000	72.7	3
IVORY COAST	60.8	9	1.250	100.0	5
IRAN	55.4	10	1.000	72.7	9
NICARAGUA	55.0	11	1.500	72.7	9
ZAMBIA	50.0	12	1.500	100.0	8
PHILIPPINES	49.0	13	1.375	99.9	7
ZAIRE	44.0	14	1.750	99.0	11
GUINEA	40.0	15	NA	NA	NA
BOLIVIA	25.0	16	NA	NA	NA
JAMAICA	15.6	17	NA	NA	NA
TURKEY	15.3	18	NA	NA	NA
ISRAEL	10.0	19	1.500	100.0	8
COLUMBIA	10.0	19	NA		NA
THAILAND	9.7	20	0.625	100.0	1
MALAWI	5.3	21	0.625	100.0	1
TOTAL	2433.6				

Source: World Bank: Capital Markets System.

TABLE 4.11

THE AGGRESSIVE IMAGE:
TYPE OF MAJOR EXPORT COMMODITY, 1968

COUNTRY	RANK BY AMOUNT OF LOAN	TYPE OF COMMODITY
BRAZIL	1	Coffee
ARGENTINA	2	Natural Resources/Agriculture
MEXICO	3	Petroleum/Agriculture
INDONESIA	4	Petroleum/Rubber/Agriculture
PANAMA	5	Bananas
MALAYSIA	6	Rubber/Edible Oils
PERU	7	Copper
KOREA	8	Diversified-Textiles
IVORY COAST	9	Agriculture
IRAN	10	Crude Petroleum
NICARAGUA	11	Agriculture
ZAMBIA	12	Copper
PHILIPPINES	13	Primary Commodities
ZAIRE	14	Minerals/Metals
GUINEA	15	Rubber
BOLIVIA	16	Tin Ore
JAMAICA	17	Bauxite
TURKEY	18	Primary Commodities
ISRAEL	19	Manufactures
COLUMBIA	20	Coffee
THAILAND	21	Minerals/Agriculture
MALAWI	22	Minerals/Agriculture

Sources: For specific commodities (where available), United Nations , Review of International Trade and Development, 1970. (New York: United Nations, 1970), p. 23. General categories, World Bank, World Development Indicators. (Washington, D.C. 1979), pp. 26-27.

TABLE 4.12

THE AGGRESSIVE IMAGE:
GROWTH RATE OF EXPORTS 1960-1968

COUNTRY	RANK BY AMOUNT	SPREAD	RANK BY GROWTH RATE OF EXPORTS*	GROWTH RATE (!
BRAZIL	1	4	14	(5.7)
ARGENTINA	2	8	15	(4.7)
MEXICO	3	2	13	(6.3)
INDONESIA	4	8	18	(-0.8)
PANAMA	5	6	2	(17.1)
MALAYSIA	6	5	16	(4.0)
PERU	7	10	10	(8.2)
KOREA	8	3	1	(40.1)
IVORY COAST	9	5	7	(12.1)
IRAN	10	3	8	(11.6)
NICARAGUA	11	9	6	(13.2)
ZAMBIA	12	8	5	(13.6)
PHILIPPINES	13	7	11	(7.4)
ZAIRE	14	11	NA	NA
GUINEA	15	NA	NA	NA
BOLIVIA	16	NA	3	(16.2)
JAMAICA	17	NA	19	(-4.4)
TURKEY	18	NA	NA	NA
ISRAEL	19	8	4	(13.9)
COLUMBIA	20	NA	17	(3.0)
THAILAND	21	1	12	(6.4)
MALAWI	22	1	9	(10.2)

* Ranking ranges from 1 (highest growth rate) to 19 (lowest). There are three missing cases.

Source: United Nations, Review of International Trade and Development, 1970. (New York: United Nations, 1970), p. 39.

TABLE 4.13

THE AGGRESSIVE IMAGE: DEBT SERVICE AS A PERCENTAGE OF EXPORTS - 1970

COUNTRY	RANK BY AMOUNT	RANK BY SPREAD	RANK BY % OF DS/EXPORTS*	% OF DEBT SERVICE EXPORTS
BRAZIL	1	4	17	14.1
ARGENTINA	2	8	18	21.4
MEXICO	3	2	20	23.6
INDONESIA	4	8	7	6.6
PANAMA	5	6	11	7.7
MALAYSIA	6	5	3	3.0
PERU	7	10	16	13.6
KOREA	8	3	19	22.0
IVORY COAST	9	5	8	6.7
IRAN	10	3	15	12.2
NICARAGUA	11	9	12	10.4
ZAMBIA	12	8	6	5.4
PHILIPPINES	13	7	10	7.6
ZAIRE	14	11	5	4.6
GUINEA	15	NA	NA	NA
BOLIVIA	16	NA	13	10.9
JAMAICA	17	NA	2	2.9
TURKEY	18	NA	18	21.4
ISRAEL	19	8	1	2.6
COLUMBIA	20	NA	14	11.6
THAILAND	21	1	4	3.3
MALAWI	22	1	9	7.0

* The DS is an abbreviation for Debt Service.

Source: The World Bank, World Development Report 1978. (Washington, D.C.: The World Bank, 1978), pp. 92-93.

TABLE 4.14

THE AGGRESSIVE IMAGE:
DATA ON PUBLIC RESCHEDULINGS

COUNTRY	YEAR OF RESCHEDULING
Argentina	1956
	1962
	1965
Brazil	1961
	1964
Cambodia	1972
Chile	1965
	1972
Ghana	1966
	1968
	1970
India	1968
	1971
	1972
Indonesia	1966
	1967
	1968
	1970
	1970
Pakistan	1972
Peru	1968
	1969
Turkey	1959
	1965

Source: Albert Cizauskas, "International Debt Renegotiations".

TABLE 4.15

COMPARISON OF COUNTRIES RECEIVING LOANS FROM AGGRESSIVE BANKERS ON CRITERIA SET FORTH BY CONSERVATIVE BANKERS POLITICAL INDICATORS

COUNTRY	GOVT. SANCTIONS	IRREGULAR EXECUTIVE TRANSFERS	ATTITUDE TOWARDS FDI	ATTITUDE TOWARDS MULTI-NATIONAL BANKING
Indonesia	320	1	Some restr.	Some restrictions
Panama	30	1	Encouraged	Encouraged
Malaysia	97	0	Some restr.	Some restrictions
Ivory Coast	18	0	Allowed	NA
Zambia	71	0	Some restr.	NA
Zaire	NA	NA	NA	NA
Guinea	NA	NA	NA	NA
Bolivia	82	0	Allowed	Some restrictions
Jamaica	15	0	Some restr.	Some restrictions
Turkey	126	1	Encouraged	Allowed
Israel	NA	0	Some restr.	Some restrictions
Colombia	39	1	Some restr.	Some restrictions
Thailand	35	0	Allowed	Some restrictions
Malawi	30	0	NA	NA

Sources: On government sanctions and irregular executive transfers, see Charles Taylor and Michael Hudson, *World Handbook of Political and Social Indicators*, 1972. On attitude towards foreign direct investment and multinational banking, see *Information Guide to Doing Business*, Price & Waterhouse.

TABLE 4.16

COMPARISON OF COUNTRIES RECEIVING LOANS FROM AGGRESSIVE BANKERS
ON CRITERIA SET FORTH BY CONSERVATIVE BANKERS
ECONOMIC INDICATORS:
1960-1968

COUNTRY	GNP/CAPITA	GNP GROWTH RATE	CONCENTRATION OF EXPORTS
Indonesia	97	2.6	53
Panama	602	8.0	73
Malaysia	384	5.7	42
Ivory Coast	303	7.5	NA
Zambia	325	8.3	NA
Zaire	200	2.1	44
Guinea	NA	NA	NA
Bolivia	168	5.5	52
Jamaica	498	4.0	50
Turkey	NA	NA	17
Israel	1,472	8.2	NA
Colombia	292	4.8	63
Thailand	164	7.3	NA
Malawi	58	3.4	NA

Sources: United Nations, *Review of International Trade and Development*, 1970 and United Nations, *Transnational Corporations in World Development*.

TABLE 4.17

COMPARISON OF COUNTRIES RECEIVING LOANS FROM AGGRESSIVE BANKERS ON CRITERIA SET FORTH BY CONSERVATIVE BANKERS SOCIAL INDICATORS 1968

COUNTRY	LITERACY RATE
Indonesia	43
Panama	73
Malaysia	41
Ivory Coast	20
Zambia	NA
Zaire	35
Guinea	10
Bolivia	32
Jamaica	85
Turkey	45
Israel	90
Colombia	65
Thailand	70
Malawi	8

Source: *UNESCO STATISTICAL HANDBOOK, 1968*

TABLE 4.18

COMPARISON OF COUNTRIES RECEIVING LOANS FROM CONSERVATIVE BANKERS ON CRITERIA SET FORTH BY AGGRESSIVE BANKERS

NAME OF COUNTRY	TYPE OF COMMODITY	GROWTH RATE OF EXPORTS 1960-1968	DEBT SERVICE AS % OF EXPORTS	PUBLIC DEBT RESCHEDULING	% OF IRREGULAR TRANSFERS
Ecuador	Primary	4.5	9.0	NO	1
Egypt	Primary	5.7	28.7	NO	1
Taiwan	Manufacturing/ Textiles	10.0	24.0	NO	0

SOURCES: Type of commodity, growth rate of exports: United Nations, *Review of International Trade and Development*, 1970. Debt-Service as a percentage of exports: World Bank. *World Development Indicators.* Debt-rescheduling, Cizauskas, "International Debt Renegotiations." Number of irregular transfers: *The World Handbook of Political and Social Indicators.*

TABLE 4.19

THE MERGED IMAGE
TOTAL AMOUNTS LOANED, MODAL SPREADS, PERCENTS AND RANKINGS:

Country	($MIL) Amount	Rank by amount	Modal Spread	%	Rank
Mexico	6486.00	1	0.750	19.3	6
Brazil	4868.00	2	0.750	50.8	4
Korea	3792.60	3	0.750	65.9	3
Philippines	2428.50	4	1.000	19.3	18
Indonesia	2264.90	5	0.750	27.3	5
Venezuela	2022.70	6	0.625	58.6	1
Argentina	1667.50	7	0.750	17.9	7
Chile	1402.00	8	1.000	16.8	19
Malaysia	1218.19	9	0.625	24.6	2
Nigeria	1100.00	10	1.000	100.0	14
Taiwan	1021.60	11	1.375	15.2	26
Ecuador	768.10	12	0.875	67.6	11
Algeria	743.10	13	0.875	26.9	13
Turkey	702.00	14	1.750	57.9	32
Iran	660.00	15	0.875	46.9	12
Peru	656.40	16	1.375	59.1	25
Colombia	553.00	17	0.750	63.2	2
Ivory Coast	468.50	18	2.000	29.8	37
Panama	386.50	19	1.375	77.6	24
Malawi	337.00	20	1.875		34
Uruguay	290.00	21	1.250		23
Costa Rica	272.50	22	0.875	84.2	10
Thailand	270.00	23	1.000	22.2	17
Dominican Republic	240.00	24	1.250	97.8	23
Bolivia	230.00	25	1.500	67.3	29
Tunisia	225.00	26	1.125	62.4	22
Burma	187.60	27	2.250	44.2	40
Gabon	180.00	28	2.000	44.4	36
Trinidad and Tobago	173.00	29	1.000	86.7	15
Pakistan	145.50	30	1.750	76.2	31
UAE	100.00	31	1.125	100.0	20
Singapore	99.3	32	NA	NA	NA
Cyprus	85.0	33	1.000	52.8	16
Jordan	69.0	34	1.500	78.2	28

TABLE 4.19 (Continued)

THE MERGED IMAGE
TOTAL AMOUNTS LOANED, MODAL SPREADS, PERCENTS AND RANKINGS:

Country	($MIL) Amount	Rank by amount	Modal Spread	%	Rank
Senegal	60.0	35	2.100	100.0	38
Liberia	60.0	35	1.500	100.0	29
Papua New Guinea	60.0	35	0.850	58.3	8
Sri Lanka	50.0	36	0.875	100.0	9
Madagascar	44.6	37	2.125	22.4	39
Honduras	35.0	38	1.125	99.9	21
Jamaica	32.0	39	2.000	100.0	35
Swaziland	28.0	40	1.750	100.0	30
Lesotho	20.0	41	1.750	100.0	30
India	20.0	41	1.000	100.0	14
Ethiopia	14.0	42	1.875	100.0	33
Tanzania	12.0	43	1.500	100.0	27
Cameroon	8.8	44	NA	NA	NA
Egypt	8.0	45	NA	NA	NA
TOTAL:	50949.2				

TABLE 4.20

THE MERGED IMAGE
RELATIONSHIP BETWEEN AMOUNT AND GROSS DOMESTIC PRODUCT
1970-1976

Country	Rank by Amount	Rank by GDP Growth Rate	GDP Growth Rate (%)
Mexico	1	16	5.5
Brazil	2	2	10.6
Korea	3	3	10.3
Philippines	4	12	6.3
Indonesia	5	6	8.3
Venezuela	6	17	5.3
Argentina	7	25	3.2
Chile	8	33	-1.2
Malaysia	9	7	7.8
Nigeria	10	9	7.4
Taiwan	11	7	7.8
Ecuador	12	1	10.7
Algeria	13	13	6.2
Turkey	14	10	7.2
Iran	15	5	8.9
Peru	16	15	5.7
Colombia	17	11	6.5
Ivory Coast	18	11	6.5
Panama	19	18	5.2
Malawi	20	5	8.9
Uruguay	21	30	0.7
Costa Rica	22	11	6.5
Thailand	23	11	6.5
Dominican Republic	24	5	8.9
Bolivia	25	14	6.0
Tunisia	26	4	9.4
Burma	27	24	3.3
Trinidad and Tobago	30	23	3.5
Pakistan	31	22	3.6
Singapore	33	5	8.9
Jordan	35	19	5.1
Senegal	36	5	8.9
Liberia	36	26	2.9
Sri Lanka	37	26	2.9

TABLE 4.20 (Continued)

THE MERGED IMAGE
RELATIONSHIP BETWEEN AMOUNT AND GROSS DOMESTIC PRODUCT
1970-1976

Country	Rank by Amount	Rank by GDP Growth Rate	GDP Growth Rate (%)
Madagascar	38	32	0.3
Honduras	39	26	2.9
Jamaica	40	31	0.5
Lesotho	42	20	4.3
India	42	27	2.7
Ethiopia	43	28	2.5
Tanzania	44	21	4.2
Cameroon	45	27	2.7
Egypt	46	8	7.6

Source: The World Bank, World Development Indicators, 1978

TABLE 4.21

THE MERGED IMAGE
RELATIONSHIP BETWEEN AMOUNT LOANED AND CONTROL OF THE INFLATION RATE BY LDC'S
AVERAGE ANNUAL RATE OF INFLATION 1970-1976

Country	Rank by Amount	Rank by Inflation Rate	Inflation Rate (%)
Mexico	1	25	14.2
Brazil	2	39	26.1
Korea	3	32	17.5
Philippines	4	27	15.1
Indonesia	5	36	22.7
Venezuela	6	22	13.4
Argentina	7	31	16.3
Chile	8	41	273.6
Malaysia	9	4	7.0
Nigeria	10	30	16.1
Taiwan	11	20	11.9
Ecuador	12	23	13.6
Algeria	13	26	14.8
Turkey	14	34	19.8
Iran	15	37	25.2
Peru	16	29	15.6
Colombia	17	35	20.7
Ivory Coast	19	16	11.0
Panama	20	17	11.2
Malawi	21	13	9.8
Uruguay	22	40	70.5
Costa Rica	23	24	13.7
Thailand	24	15	10.3
Dominican Republic	25	9	8.9
Bolivia	26	38	52.9
Tunisia	27	5	7.7
Burma	28	30	16.1
Trinidad and Tobago	30	33	18.8
Pakistan	31	28	15.2
Singapore	33	7	8.1
Jordan	35	11	9.6
Senegal	36	21	12.1
Liberia	36	15	10.3
Papua New Guinea	36	6	7.8

TABLE 4.21 (Continued)

THE MERGED IMAGE
RELATIONSHIP BETWEEN AMOUNT LOANED AND CONTROL OF THE INFLATION RATE BY LDC'S
AVERAGE ANNUAL RATE OF INFLATION 1970-1976

Country	Rank by Amount	Rank by Inflation Rate	Inflation Rate (%)
Sri Lanka	37	18	11.5
Madagascar	38	14	10.2
Honduras	39	3	5.5
Jamaica	40	32	17.5
Lesotho	42	8	8.8
India	42	10	9.2
Ethiopia	43	1	2.3
Tanzania	44	19	11.7
Cameroon	45	12	9.7
Egypt	46	2	5.2

Source: The World Bank, World Development Indicators, 1978

TABLE 4.22

THE MERGED IMAGE
RELATIONSHIP BETWEEN AMOUNT AND REDUCTION IN PUBLIC EXPENDITURES
REDUCTION IN EXPENDITURES FOR SOCIAL WELFARE 1970-1977

Country	Rank by Amount	Rank by Expenditure	Percent (%)
Mexico	1	10	-1.76
Brazil	2	11	-1.41
Korea	3	24	0.04
Venezuela	6	2	-4.29
Argentina	7	15	-0.53
Chile	8	5	-2.90
Iran	15	17	-0.44
Peru	16	21	-0.10
Malawi	21	6	-2.56
Uruguay	22	1	-7.29
Costa Rica	23	18	-0.41
Thailand	24	19	-0.36
Bolivia	26	27	0.86
Tunisia	27	3	-3.75
Burma	28	9	-2.01
Pakistan	31	22	-0.06
Singapore	33	25	0.74
Jordan	35	8	-2.30
Liberia	36	20	-0.13
Papua New Guinea	36	23	-0.01
Sri Lanka	37	29	7.02
Madagascar	38	6	-0.56
Honduras	39	7	-2.50
Jamaica	40	14	-0.56
Lesotho	42	12	-1.03
India	42	13	-0.60
Ethiopia	43	16	-0.49
Tanzania	44	26	-0.81
Egypt	46	4	-3.47

Source: IMF, Government Finance Statistics Handbook, 1980

TABLE 4.23
THE MERGED IMAGE
PUBLIC DEBT RESCHEDULINGS 1970-1978

COUNTRY	YEAR:
Chile*	1972
	1974
	1975
Ghana	1970
	1974
India*	1971-1978
Indonesia*	1970
Pakistan*	1972
	1973
	1974
Peru*	1978
Turkey*	1978
Sierra Leone	1977
Zaire	1976
	1977

*Means that these countries received loans from the bankers during the second period of lendin

Source: Albert Cizauskas, "International Debt Renegotiations: Lessons from the Past." World Development Vol. 7 (1979): pp. 199-210.

IV: REFERENCES

[1] See Organization for Economic Cooperation and Development, Development Cooperation, 1979. (Paris: OECD, 1979): p. 253.

[2] See United Nations Economic and Social Council, Transnational Corporations in World Development: A Reexamination. (New York: United Nations, 1978. E/C.10/38).

[3] Defined as countries with GNP's per capita of less than $500.

[4] Irving Friedman, The Emerging Role of Private Bankers in the Developing World. (New York: Citicorp Publications, 1977): p. 63.

[5] Salomon Brothers, A Review of Bank Performance, 1987 (1987): p. 87.

V: BAKER, BRADLEY, AND BEYOND

Secretary Baker: We are not offering the banks any sort of bailout.

Senator Lugar: You are offering them an invitation to continue in the game, in essence?

Secretary Baker: Hopefully, we are trying to offer them some leadership with respect to a very, very difficult international problem that is of great significance, we think, to the U.S.

One thing we might be able to provide here is some governmental leadership toward helping to accomplish or at least convince some of these major debtor nations that the way out is to adopt the same kinds of growth-oriented economic reforms that have brought prosperity to this country.

Kassebaum: To which countries has this been done (increase in lending of 2.5%)

Baker: Well, there have been no new commercial loans as yet. We think that there will be.

Economic Summit, Latin Debt and the Baker Plan. Hearings Before the Committee on Foreign Relations, United State Senate, 20 May 1986.

While a great deal has changed since the original research was conducted for this study, the bankers, particularly the U.S. bankers, are obviously still one of the key players in current debt strategies, along with the International Monetary Fund, the World Bank, and the industrialized country governments. But, as Secretary Baker's responses point out the bankers are not willing players.

While the exposure of the U.S. banks to all oil-importing countries increased from $66.2 billion in 1980 to $125.8 billion in 1985, [1] **private** long term lending to developing countries reached a peak of $121 billion in 1981. (See Figure One). According to Morgan Guaranty's World Financial Markets , "there is no evidence that *net* voluntary lending to countries that have experienced debt problems has resumed since 1982." [2] In fact, according to this publication, "banks have curtailed net new lending even to developing countries that have avoided debt problems." [3]

Recent increases in loan loss reserves by the major U.S. banks, such as Citicorp's $3 billion and Bank of America's $1.1 billion set asides indicate that the banks are unlikely to lend new money and may make the banks more aggressive in debt renegotiations. Instead of major players, the bankers have relegated themselves to the sidelines in the hopes that industrialized governments and multilateral institutions such as the IMF and the World Bank, can keep the game alive.

What can be drawn from the images of creditworthiness and the lending behavior analyzed in chapter three that might help to explain the bankers' current lending behavior, and what are the implications of this new behavior?

Perhaps what is most interesting about the images of creditworthiness outlined above are the *omissions*, the factors that were not examined by the bankers in the period from 1972-1980. The six banks represented in this work, seemed to take a ceteris paribus view of the international environment, that is that there would not be major structural changes in the international environment for lending. And yet it has been primarily factors external to domestic policy makers control that precipitated the current crisis. The prolonged recession in the industrialized countries and high real interest rates during the early 1980's, combined with worsening terms of trade for the LDC's led to the crisis of 1982. In the past five years, decreases in commodity prices coupled with increased protectionist sentiment in the industrialized countries, particularly in the U.S., have put further strains on many already overburdened debtor governments.

The bankers gambled that growth and open markets in the industrialized countries would ensure repayment of their loans. The developing country borrowers in particular, have lost heavily on that bet.

This shortsighted view of the lending environment resembles the boom-bust cycle described best by Charles Kindleberger.[4] Kindleberger points out that the boom-bust cycle of lending where bankers overextend themselves by matching the lending behavior of other players and underestimate downturns in the international economy, has occurred several times throughout history. The boom has inevitably been followed by a bust, according to Kindleberger's explanation because of the lack of a lender of last resort. If bankers behavior is best explained by this argument, is the crash described by Kindleberger inevitable? Or can what has been termed "cooperation without reform"[5] lead to a solution of the debt crisis.

While there are important differences between the

debt and defaults of the 1930's and the current problems, particularly that International lending in the 1930's was financed primarily through bonds, and there was no obvious lender of last resort, like the IMF, some of the similarities are striking. A recent analysis which sought to determine the factors leading to default in the 1930's and compare the period of the 1930's to the current period concluded that factors outside of any one government's control may be the most important reasons leading to a default. According to the authors of this study, "In neither period can the problems experienced by external debtors be attributed exclusively to domestic economic and political developments; rather they must be linked to disturbances in the world economy including, in each instance, real interest rate shocks, commodity price fluctuations, and exceptionally severe recessions in industrialized regions." [6]

The authors of "Debt and Default in the 1930: Causes and Consequences," also point out, however, that the economic shocks experienced during the 1930's were much more severe than any current disturbances. What happened to commodity prices during this period illustrates the severity of the downturn. " Between 1929 and 1930 the fall in average annual dollar prices ranged from nearly 20% for wheat and tin to 30% for cotton, sugar and silk and 40% for rubber." [7]

Several plans have been put forth in the last few years which were intended to reduce the risk of default and regularize debt repayments.

In 1985, at the Annual meeting of the World Bank and the

International Monetary Fund in Seoul, Korea, Treasury Secretary Baker unveiled the Program for Sustained Growth, also known as the Baker Plan. This plan called for structural reform in the debtor countries and increased lending by the major commercial banks. The debtor countries were to institute market oriented policy reforms including reducing public expenditures, restraining wages, removing subsidies, devaluing their currencies and liberalizing trade regimes. The commercial banks were to respond to these adjustments with new capital. Specifically, the Plan contained the following components:

1. The commercial banks would increase their lending over a three year period by $20 billion and their exposure by 2.5% a year, to fifteen countries (later expanded to seventeen countries).

2. An increase of $9 billion would be provided to major debtors from the World Bank and the Inter-American Development Bank, also over a three year period.

3. The World Bank's Multilateral Investment Guarantee Agency would provide guarantees to boost foreign direct investment in the major debtor countries.

Notwithstanding favorable reports from the Treasury Department, the Baker Plan has had only marginal impacts on the debtor countries. While many of the major debtor countries have begun to initiate and implement major structural reforms, the private banks have not increased their lending even to the level envisioned by this Plan. The Plan has failed because it relies on voluntary lending by the commercial banks and it offers no real incentives for the banks to increase their lending. Instead of increased lending, the banks have used the period between major crises to withdraw further from new loans to the debtor countries. Many of the banks recently have dramatically increased their loan loss reserves, further indicating that new loans to developing country debtors are not likely to materialize.

The banks have concluded that multilateral institutions such as the International Monetary Fund and the World Bank should now be the major players in providing new capital and monitoring structural reforms.[8] Meanwhile, many of the debtor countries have instituted policy reforms but have not been able to attract the new capital needed for growth and investment.

In response to the Baker Plan, Senator Bill Bradley put forth a plan to deal with the debt problem. The Bradley Plan announced in Zurich in June of 1986 recognizes the links between growth and debt in the developing countries and trade and employment in the industrialized countries, and shifts some of the burdens associated with mounting debts away from the debtor countries.

According to Bradley, "In order to repay their debts, Latin American countries have cut imports...U.S. industries and farms find it impossible to sell their products in Latin American markets...U.S. exports to Latin America shrank by one third during the first year of the debt crisis. Altogether, one million U.S. workers have lost their jobs as a direct result of the debt crisis." [9]

The three tiered approach of the Bradley Plan includes:

1. Interest rate relief of three points per year for three years to countries which institute policy reforms;

2. A three percent write down and some outright forgiveness of principal for eligible countries; and

3. Three billion in new structural adjustment monies for eligible countries.

Not surprisingly, the Bradley Plan was met with hostility by the bankers who are solidly against any forgiveness of principal or any solutions which deal with debtor countries on anything but a case-by-case basis .

Lawrence Brainard, the chief international economist at Bankers Trust stated that, "It is a step in the wrong direction, as it sends the message that if you as a country do not perform, you will be rewarded." [10]

This proposal is a step in the right direction in that it recognizes the importance of shifting the burdens from debtor countries to industrialized countries and that the banks themselves need to take some of the debt burden which has occurred in part, from their poor judgments. Yet even the Bradley Plan is not a realistic solution to the debt crisis. Banks cannot be forced either to increase lending or to forgive old debt.

More recent developments on the debt front, such as exchanging debt-for-equity offer little relief for debtors.

In the debt-for-equity approach an investor, usually a

multinational corporation, purchases debt at a discount, (ranging from from ten cents on the dollar for Bolivian debt to 57 cents for Mexican debt,[11]) which is then exchanged by the debtor's central bank for local currency and then invested in the debtor country. A recent example of an innovate debt swap involved a conservation group purchasing $650,000 in Bolivian debt in exchange for 4 million acres of tropical rain forest in the Amazon.[12]

This "debt for nature" swap, however, like many of the debt-for- equity swaps, retired only a small amount of Bolivia's $4 billion debt. While more traditional debt-for-equity swaps have been somewhat successful in Chile, Mexico, and the Philippines,[13] the total amount of debt which has been exchanged through debt-for-equity mechanisms was estimated at only $5 billion in 1986, out of a total of $900 billion of LDC debt.

While there are potential benefits for U.S. banks and multinationals including: reducing or shifting exposure and various tax benefits,[14] the swaps do little to assist the developing economies. They are potentially inflationary; they are seen by many as a way for investors who would have invested anyway, to buy into a developing country at a discount, and they further increase the dependence of the developing countries on outside investors.

None of the current strategies, proposed solutions or growing market responses are comprehensive enough to alleviate the debt burden and ensure that growth within the developing countries will be forthcoming. The debt problems of the developing countries will not disappear. The ability of the developing country borrowers, both politically and economically, to repay their debts is more in question now than in any period since the crises of 1982.

While the exports of the developing country borrowers have increased in volume terms from 1983-85, in dollar terms, "the debtors on average have garnered no increase," [15] in their export earnings. Export prices for developing country products continued to decline during 1986. Since 1981, prices for primary commodities have dropped dramatically (See Figure Two). Declines in the price of oil (See Figure Three) pushed Mexico, once again, to the brink of default. While the arrangement between the Mexican government and the IMF signed in the summer of 1986 is unprecedented in that the IMF for the first time linked lending to the price of exports, (agreeing to lend additional money if the price of oil drops below $9 a barrel), the total package ensures only that Mexico will be able to repay interest for another year. Brazil suspended interest payments on its more than $100 billion debt in February, 1987, as it became clear to this government's new democratic leaders, that the domestic political costs of continuing to service its massive debt were higher than possible repercussions from international lenders.

Living standards within the developing countries also continue to erode. In 1985, per capita G.N.P. was below 1982 levels for most of the Latin American borrowers. (See Table One).

The current structure organized to deal with the debt problem is extremely fragile. Unless a solution is developed

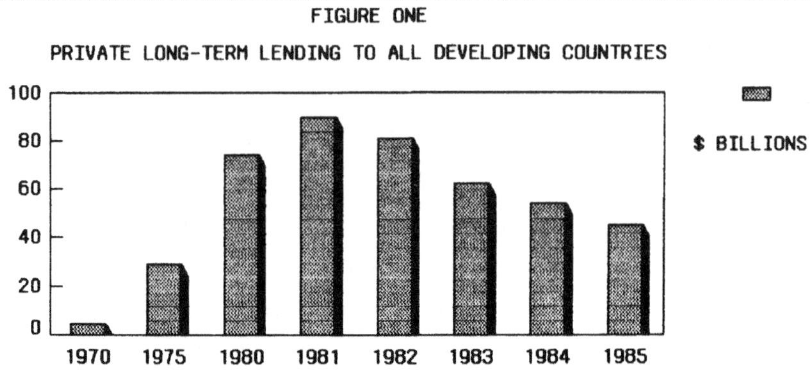

Sources: World Bank (1986) p. xx, (1981) p. 52.

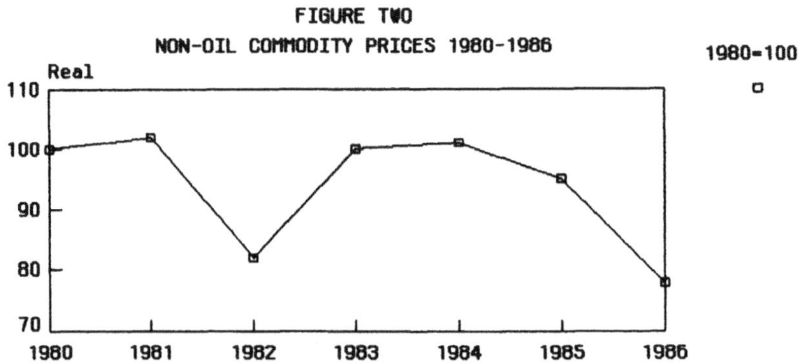

Source: World Financial Markets, February 1986, p. 5.

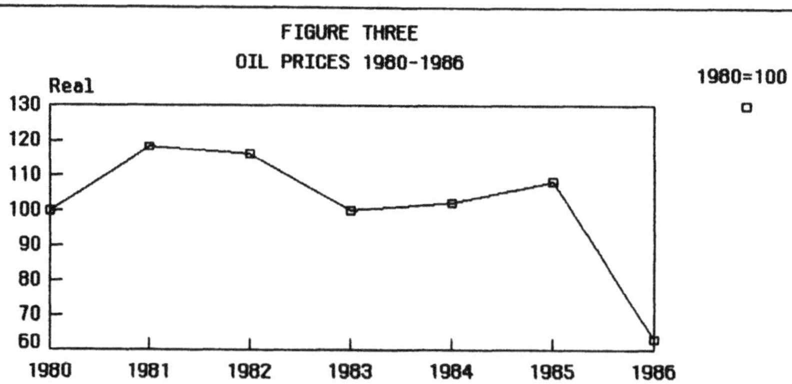

Source: World Financial Markets, February, 1986, p. 5.

Table One

Real GNP Per Capita
% Change From Peak Period 1982-1985

Argentina	-16.8
Bolivia	-28.4
Brazil	- 3.4
Chile	14.4
Columbia	0.9
Ecuador	- 6.6
Mexico	- 3.0
Peru	-14.2
Uruguay	-18.0
Venezuela	-19.3
10 Major Latin American Debtors	- 7.2

Source: World Financial Markets, February, 1986, p.6

which addresses the long term financial needs of the developing countries by working simultaneously on actually reducing the debt burden of the developing countries and increasing the access of the developing countries to the industrialized countries markets, the simmering crisis of debt could easily erupt into a system wide disaster affecting both developed and developing countries.

The costs of the current impasse are shared by populations both in the developing and industrialized countries. A report by the Joint Economic Committee of the U.S. Senate released in May of 1986 documents the impact of the debt crisis both on employment in the U.S. and increasing impoverishment in the debtor concluding that "more than one million American jobs had been lost because the debt crisis forced debtor nations to reduce their imports of U.S. products."[16]

Until there is a recognition by leaders in the United States and other major industrial countries that the debt problem is not a financial problem but rather a political and economic problem affecting the entire international community, solutions will continue to be stop-gap in nature and short sighted. The inability of the developing countries to sustain growth and the increasing poverty resulting from austerity plans impedes not only the development prospects of these countries but directly affects the growth and future prosperity of the industrialized countries and their populations.

V: REFERENCES

[1] A Review of Bank Performance, 1987 Edition, **Salomon Brothers, Inc., (1987): p. 90.**
[2] World Financial Markets, "International Bank Lending Trends." (July 1985): p. 1

[3] Ibid.

[4] See Charles P. Kindleberger, Manias, Panics and Crises (New York: Basic Books, 1978).

[5] See Miles Kalher, The Politics of International Debt, (Ithaca: Cornell University Press, 1986).

[6]. Barry Eichengreen and Richard Portes, "Debt and Default in the 1930's: Causes and Consequences." (London: Centre for Economic Policy Research Discussion Paper No. 75), (October 1985): p. i.

[7]. Ibid., p. 15

[8]. See "LDC Debt: Debt Relief or Market Solutions?" World Financial Markets, (September, 1986).

[9] Senator Bill Bradley, "A Proposal for Third World Debt Management," Lausanne: Switzerland (29 June, 1986,): p.1.

---

10. Erik Ipsen, "Bill Bradley's Game Plan." Institutional Investor (February 1987): p. 70.

11 See Paul Volker, "Illustrative Calculations of Examples of Hypothetical Debt Relief." Unpublished Paper from the Federal Reserve, (November 1986): Appendix One.

12 See "A Debt Swap of a Different Nature for Bolivia," New York Times, (14 July, 1987), Business Section.

13. See Gary Hector, "Swaps Can Shrink Latin Debt--A Little." Fortune (18 August 1986).

14 The secondary market is growing, despite possible regulatory problems associated with debt-for-equity swaps. U.S. banking regulations require American banks to write off loans if they are sold at too much below face value. However, see Treasury Secretary Baker's discussion of this potential problem in his testimony before the U.S. Senate Foreign Relations Committee in, "Economic Summit, Latin Debt and the Baker Plan."

15 World Financial Markets, "The Baker Initiative: The Perspective of the Banks." (February 1986): p. 2.

16. Cited in Hearings Before the Committee on Foreign Relations of the United States Senate, "Economic Summit, Latin Debt and the Baket Plan," (May 1986): p.24.

APPENDIX ONE: THE SIMULATIONS

The simulator which was used to represent the bankers' images of creditworthiness was developed by Chuck Rieger and Milt Grinberg at the University of Maryland. The simulator (formally called the mechanism simulator) encapsulates two important notions about knowledge representation: the concept of the common sense algorithm, (CSA), and the notion of spontaneous computations (SC). Commonsense algorithmic knowledge includes dynamic problem-solving knowledge and is, according to Rieger, "that which relates to actions, states and the notions of causality and enablement in the activities we all do ... day-to-day." [1] This type of knowledge is represented in the simulator by events and links, or conditions and causal connections, which were designed to express the notions of direct causality, indirect causality and ceteris paribus conditions (also called gating).

In building the CSA, Rieger and Grinberg, attempted to identify "a small number of cause-effect relationships which are necessary and sufficient for connecting together events into larger patterns which then reflect the application of a mechanism." [2] The simulator contains three events which represent conditions of the images: states, statechanges and actions.

A state is a static condition or a representation of a piece of information or state of affairs which already exists in the decision environment. A statechange, the second type of event, is a "changing condition with respect to some continuous attribute." An example of a statechange variable would be inflation. The third event is the action event. An action generates some type of force or change: actions cause states.

These three events or categories are connected by causal links or relationships. These relationships serve to connect the events into large data structures. (See Diagram One).

There are eight causal links in the CSA. The links which are the causal connectors between events represent different types of causal relationships. The first link, appropriately enough, is called : CAUSE. It is the primary cause-effect link in the CSA. It is employed when there is a direct cause and effect relationship between states and actions. Only actions can cause events; the caused event is either a state or a statechange. There are actually two versions of this causal link both reflecting a different time dimension. One-shot causality (OS-CAUSE), "predicts that the one-time existence of the causing action causes some state or statechange to some into and remain in existence until something else causes it to cease to exist." [3] The second time dimension of causality is termed continuous causality (C-CAUSE). There is a major difference between the two causal links. In the case of C-CAUSE, (with either the state or the statechange as the caused event), the cause is continuously required to maintain the existence of the state or the statechange.

Associated with the cause link is an additional concept, the notion of a gate. In the simulator, a causal relationship between events cannot exist until all conditions in the

DIAGRAM ONE

EVENTS AND LINKS

ENABLEMENT

S= STATE A= ACTION

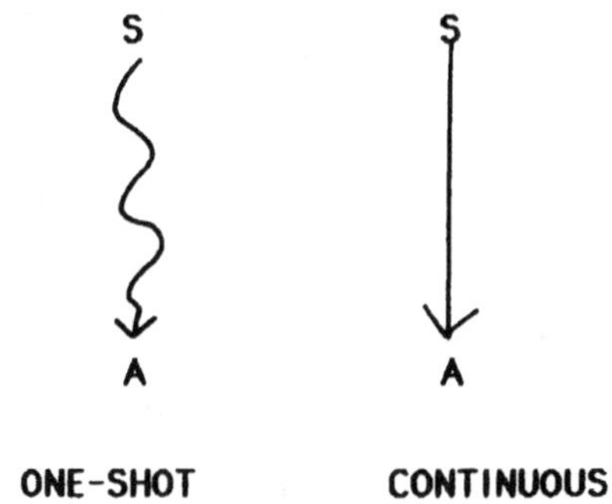

ANTAGONISM

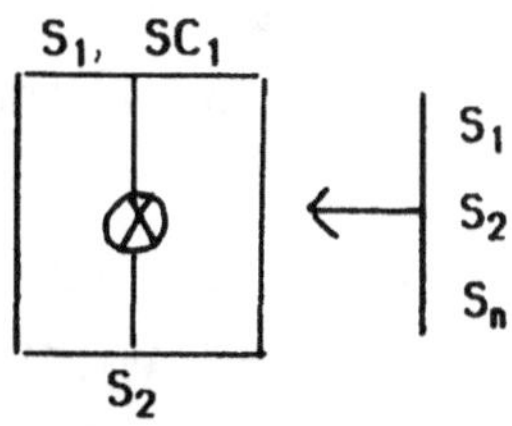

DIAGRAM ONE: CONTINUED

CAUSALITY

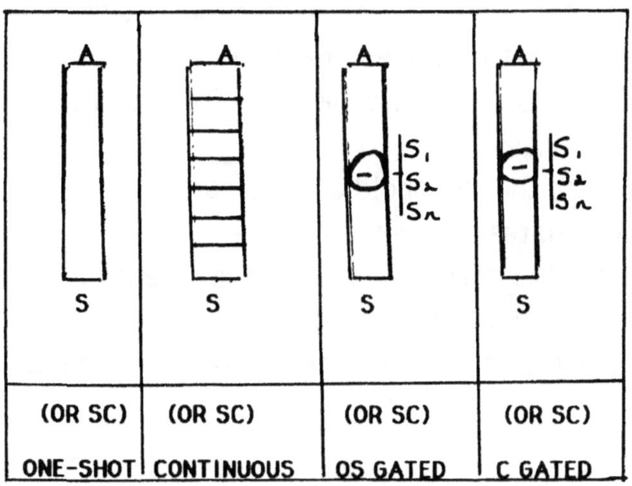

EQUIVALENCE

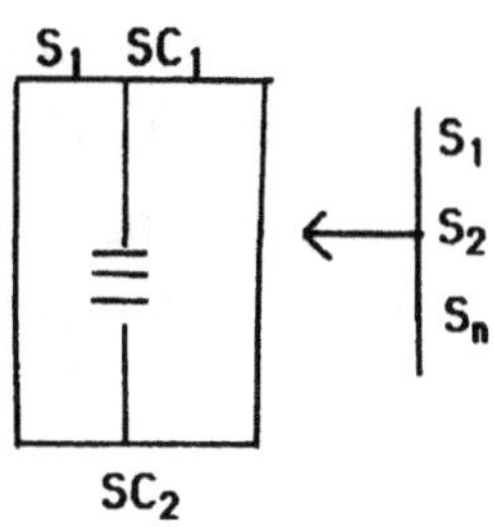

environment are correct. This represent the idea of a gate; when ceteris paribus holds, the link will be activated.

The second link is the statecouple. It is used when the causal relationship between events exists, but is indirect. In other words, the intervening causal structure is not known. According to Rieger and Grinberg, this link frequently amounts to " a kind of inferring between alternate descriptions of the same underlying condition; using different points of view which are causally related." [4]

The third link reflects the notion of equivalence between conditions while the fourth represents the conceptual opposite, antagonism. States or statechanges can be equivalent when there are two ways to define or represent the same piece of information. The opposite of this notion of equivalence is antagonism. It is called when the existence of a state or statechange leads to the negation of another state or statechange. This link is used to denote that two states are mutually exclusive.

While the concept of a gate reflects an influence on an ongoing action, the concept of enablement reflects the necessary conditions that must exist before an action can proceed. Within the simulator, states enable actions (both O-CAUSE and C-CAUSE). It is in a sense the list of preconditions for a state or a statechange.

The final links are the threshold and the rate confluence. The threshold link relates states to statechanges. The threshold link captures the notion of an increase or a decrease in the statechange. It links statechanges which refer to the same scale or object which result in a net state change of an object on that scale.

The CSA while resembling production rules, has many additional components not contained in simple production rules. In the simulator, pieces of causal information (represented using the CSA) are related via a spontaneous computation (SC) system. The SC is like a watcher or a demon. It scans the entire data base (which is composed of the events related by links) to see what should be triggered by each link. In other words, "it causes computations to be invoked or aborted not because some other part of the model has requested so, but because a computations' 'trigger pattern' has matched some condition in the system." [5] This notion represents a substantial advance over demand based hierarchical systems. Computations are not ordered in any preconceived way but are triggered spontaneously, based on the causal patterns.

The simulator then actually consists of three parts: the initial representation of a chunk of information (via linked events); a spontaneous computation model of each link in the initial representation; and finally the running of the model which involves establishing those conditions which set the model in motion (INITIAL CONDITIONS-IC), and a trigger. Both of these last two components can be changed from one run to the next.

The Common Sense Algorithm, along with the notion of Spontaneous Computations, correspond to the information processing concepts of frames, structured information and a central processor. The entire system can be considered a control structure. (See Newell, 1975).

The mechanism simulator was used to represent the

decision-making structure of international bankers on LDC creditworthiness.

THE IMAGES

Conservative Image: Example Data Base and Run

```
($ Mechanism ' (
(Name Conservative-Image
(Events
(1 S (Borrowers market))
(2 S (Banks need new source of demand))
(3 A (Demand for external capital LDCs))
(4 S (Assessment of CW))
(5 A (Political risk analysis))
(6 A (Economic risk analysis))
(7 S (No negative shift in govt. attitude toward PDI govt. open to foreign investment))
(8 S (Govt. open to US FDI))
(9 S (GNP per capita > 250))
(10 S (If GNP growth rate > 2.5%))
(11 S (Commitment to welfare services))
(12 S (Commitment toward multinational banking))
(13 S (If political stability > five years))
(14 S (If regular transfer of power > five years))
(15 S (If terrorism under control))
(16 S (If debt primarily bilateral))
(17 S (Loan to LDC
(Links
(c-cause (5 13))
(s-equiv ( 1 2))
(c-enable (4 6))
(c-cause (3 4))
```

```
(c-cause (6 10))
(c-cause (6 9))
(c-cause (5 12))
(c-enable (4 5))
(c-cause (5 11))
(c-cause (5 13))
(c-cause (5 7))
(c-cause (5 8))
(c-cause (3 14))
(s-equiv (13 14))
(s-equiv (13 15))
(c-cause (6 16))
(initial world 1))
(trigger 3))
```

The Aggressive Image: Example Data Base and Run

```
($ Mechanism ' (
(Name Aggressive-Image)
(Events
(1 S (Borrowers market))
(2 S (Banks need new sources of demand))
(3 S (Demand for external capital by LDC's))
(4 S (Assessment of CW))
(5 S (Economic risk analysis))
(6 S (Political risk analysis))
(7 S (If major export commodity either ag. or nat resource))
(8 S ( If govt. attitude towards FDI positive and no anti MNC
        sentiment))
(9 S (If percentage of DS burden < 15 percent of exports))
```

```
(10 S (If stable govt > five years))
(11 S (If no rescheduling of public debt in five years))
(12 S (If DSR low))
(13 S (If govt. in control of labor))
(14 S (If labor uprisings))
(Links
(c-cause (3 4))
(c-enable (4 5))
(c-cause (6 10))
(c-enable (4 6))
(c-cause (6 11))
(c-cause (6 8))
(Antag (14 15))
(c-cause (5 7))
(c-cause (5 9))
(c-cause (5 12))
(c-cause (5 14))
(s-equiv (1 2))
(s-equiv (2 13))
(Initial world 1)
(Trigger 3)
```

The Merged Image Example Data Base and Run

```
($ Mechanism '(
(Name Merged-Image)
(Events
(1 S (lenders market)
(2 A (Reassessment of LDC loans))
```

```
(3 S (Reexamination of purpose of loans))
(4 A (Demand for external capital by LDC's))
(5 S (Assessment of CW))
(6 A (Political risk analysis))
(7 A (Economic risk analysis))
(8 S (If govt in good standing with IMF))
(9 S (If govt rs with US))
(10 S (Commitment to domestic adjustment policies))
(11 S (If no public reschedulings))
(12 S (Commitment to cuts in public spending))
(13 S (If growth in domestic production))
(14 S (If no negative shift in attitude toward FDI))
(15 S (If inflation under control))
(16 S (If loan contributed to development of energy resources
      domestic or nr development))
(17 S (Loan to LDC))
(Links
(c-cause (4 5))
(c-enable (5 6))
(c-cause (2 3))
(c-cause (6 8))
(c-enable (5 7))
(c-enable (1 2))
(c-cause (6 9))
(c-cause (6 11))
(c-cause (6 10))
(c-cause (6 12))
(c-cause (7 16))
(c-cause (7 15))
```

```
(c-cause (6 14))
(c-cause (7 13))
(Initial-world 1)
(Trigger 4)
```

---

[1] Chuck Rieger, "One System for Two Tasks." University of Maryland, TR-435, (1975): p. 1.

[2] Ibid., p. 6.

[3] Ibid., p. 17.

[4] Ibid., p. 19.

[5] Ibid., p. 33.

BIBLIOGRAPHY

Abelson, Robert P. "Concepts for Representing Mundane Reality in Plans." In Representation and Understanding., edited by D. Bobrow and A. Collins, New York: Academic Press, 1975.

____. "The Structure of Belief Systems." In Computer Models of Thought and Language., edited by Roger C. Schank and K. Colby. San Francisco: W.H. Freeman, 1973.

Ahmed, M.M. "The Developing Countries and Access to Financial Markets." Finance and Development (December 1976): 26-30.

Aliber, Robert. "Living With LDC Debt." Lloyd's Bank Review. 126 (October 1977): 34-44.

Alker, H.R. and Cheryl Christensen, "From Causal Models to Artificial Intelligence." In Experimentation and Simulation in Political Science, edited by J. LaPonce and P. Smoker. Toronto: University of Toronto Press, 1972.

Angelini, Anthony, M. Eng and Francis Lees. International Lending, Risks and the Euromarkets. New York: John Wiley and Sons, 1979.

Aronson, Jonathan ed. Debt and the Less-Developed Countries. Boulder, Colorado: Westview Presss, 1979.

____. Money and Power: Banks and the World Monetary System. Beverly Hills, California: Sage Publications, 1977.

Association of Reserve City Bankers. Country Exposure Measurement and the Reporting Practices of Member Banks. Washington, D.C.: American Bankers Association, 1977.

Axelrod, Robert ed. The Structure of Decision: The Cognitive Maps of Political Elites. Princeton, New Jersey: Princeton University Press, 1976.

Balassa, Bela. Adjustment Policies in Developing Countries, 1979-83: An Update. Washington, D.C.: The World Bank, 1984.

Balogh, Thomas. "The Transfer Problem Revisited: Analysis Between the Reparation Payment's of the 1920's and the Problem of the OPEC Surpluses." Oxford Bulletin of Economic and Statistics 41 (August 1979): 183-191.

The Banker . Various Issues.

Barr, Avron and Edward Feigenbaum, eds. The Handbook of Artificial Intelligence Vols. 1-3. Los Altos, California: William Kaufmann Inc., 1982.

Bennett, James. "Data Stories: Learning About Learning from the U.S. Experience in Vietnam." In Foreign Policy Decision Making. Edited by Donald Sylvan and Steve Chan. New York: Praeger Publishers, 1984.

Bentley, Richard. "Debt Conversion in Latin America." Columbia Journal of World Business Vol. XXI No. 3 (Fall 1986): 37-40.

Berg, Eric. "Debt Crisis: Fresh Approaches." *The New York Times* , 5 May 1987, Business Section.

______, "Markets Fail to Develop for Third-World Debt." *The New York Times*, 1 June 1987, Business Section.

Bergsten, C. Fred, William Cline and John Williamson. "Bank Lending to Developing Countries: The Policy Alternatives." Policy Analyses in International Economics 10. Washington, D.C.: Institute for International Economic, 1985.

Bienen, Henry and Mark Gersovitz. "Economic Stabilization, Conditionality and Political Stability." International Organization 39 No. 4 (Autumn 1985):

Boden, Margaret A. Artificial Intelligence and Natural Man. New York: Basic Books, 1977.

Bogdanowicz-Bindert Christine and T. Chris Canavan, "The World Bank and the International Private Sector." Columbia Journal of World Business, Vol. XXI No. 3 (all 1986): 31-35.

Brachman, Ronald and Hector Levesque, eds. Readings in Knowledge Representation. Los Altos, California: William Kaufmann, Inc., 1985.

Brainard, Lawrence. "Assessing Country Risk: How Bankers Trust Analyses Its International Risks." Paper Presented at Conference on Country Risk, New York, 30-31 October, 1980.

Bradley, Bill. "A Proposal for Third World Debt Management. " Speech Presented in Zurich, Switzerland, June, 1986.

Brooks, Harold. "Can the Baker Plan Work?" Institutional Investor. (December 1985): 279-286.

Buchanan, Bruce and Edward Shortliffe. Rule-Based Expert Systems:The MYCIN Experiments of the Stanford Heuristic Programming Project. Reading, Massachusetts: Addison Wesley Publishing Co., 1984.

Calverly, John. Country Risk Analysis. London: Butterworth, 1985.

Carbonell, Jaime. Subjective Understanding: Computer Models of Belief Systems. Ann Arbor, Michigan: UMI Press, 1981.

Centre for Development Planning, Projections and Policies. "External Financing for Development: Recent Experience and Its Implication for Policies." Journal of Development PLanning. 10 (1976): 23-54.

Cimbala, Stephen, ed. Artificial Intelligence and National Security. Lexington, Massachusetts: Lexington Books, 1987.

Cohen, Benjamin. "International Debt and Linkage Strategies: Some Foreign Policy Implications for the United States." International Organization 39 Vol. 4 (Autumn 1985):

Cline, William R. International Debt: Systemic Risk and Policy Response. Washington, D.C. : Institute for International Economics, 1984.

Collins, Allen, E. Warnock, N. Aiello and M. Miller, "Reasoning from Incomplete Knowledge." In Representation and Understanding, edited by D. Bobrow and A. Collins, New York: Academic Press, 1975.

Decoodt, Patrick. The Debt Crisis of the Third World: Some Aspects of Causes and Solutions." Columbia Journal of World Business. Vol. XXI No. 3 (Fall 1986): 3-9.

De Costa, Michael. "How Bank Lending Helps the LDC's." The Banker 130 No. 625 (October 1980): 47-51.

Delamaide, Darrell. Debt Shock: The Full Story of the World Credit Crisis. Garden City, New York: Doubleday and CVo., 1984.

Dornbusch, Rudiger. "The Debt Problem and Some Solutions." Unpublished Paper.

Eichengreen, Barry and Richard Portes. "Debt and Default in the 1930's: Causes and Consequences." Discussion Paper No. 75 (October, 1985). London: Centre for Economic Policy Research.

Euromoney. Various Issues.

Export-Import Bank, Policy Analysis Staff. "A Survey of Country Evaluation Systems in Use." (December 1976): 1-30.

Falkowski, Lawrence, ed. Psychological Models in International Politics. Boulder, Colorado: Westview Press, 1979.

Federal Reserve Bank of New York. "The Pricing of Syndicated Eurocurrency Credits." Quarterly Review 5 No. 2 (Summer 1980): 39-49.

Friedman, Irving S. "The Evolution in Country Risk Assessment. Paper Prepared for Presentation at the Conference on Country Risk, New York, 30-31 October, 1980.

——. The Emerging Role of the Private Bankers in the Developing World. New York: Citibank Publishers, 1977.

Gardner, Howard. Minds New Science: The Cognitive Revolution in the Computer Age. New York: Basic Books, 1985.

George, Alexander L. "The Causal Nexus Between Cognitive Beliefs and Decision Making Behavior: The 'Operational Code' Belief System." In Psychological Models in International Politics, edited by Lawrence Falkowski. Boulder, Colorado: Westview Press, 1979.

Goldberg, Adele. Smalltalk 80: The Interactive Programming Environment. Reading, Massachusetts: Addision-Wesley, 1984.

Goldstein, Ira and Seymour Papert. "Artificial Intelligence, Language and the Study of Knowledge." Massachusetts Institute of Technology, Artificial Intelligence Laboratory, Memo 389, (December 1976).

Goldstein, Ira. "The Genetic Graph: A Representation for the Evolution of Procedural Knowledge." In Intelligent Tuturing Systems, edited by D. Sleeman and J.S. Brown, New York: Academic Press, 1982.

Goodman, Stephen. "How the Big Banks Really Evaluate Sovereign Risk." Euromoney (February 1977): 105-110.

Griffith-Jones, Stephany. "The Growth of Multinational Banking, the Eurocurrency Market and their Effects on Developing Countries." Journal of Development Studies 6 No. 3 (April 1980): 204-223.

Grinberg, Milt and Chuck Rieger. The Mechanism Simulator Reference Manual. Department of Computer Science, University of Maryland, 1980.

Hannon, Brian and Scott Gould. "Debt/Equity Swaps Help Latin

America Out of its Debt Dilemna." Business America. 19 January 1987.

Hayes-Roth, Frederick, Donald Waterman and Douglas Lenat, eds. Building Expert Systems. Reading, Massachusetts: Addision-Wesley Publishing Company, Inc., 1983.

Hector, Gary. "Swaps Can Shrink Latin Debt-A Little." Fortune 18 August 1986.

Hearings Before the Committee on Foreign Relations, U.S Senate. "Economic Summit, Latin Debt and the Baker Plan." Alderson Reporting (May 20, 1986).

Hudson, Valerie. "Using a Rule-Based Production System to Estimate Foreign Policy Behavior: Conceptual Issues and Practical Concerns." In Artificial Intelligence and National Security, edited by Stephen Cimbala. Lexington, Massachusetts: Lexington Books, 1987.

Ipsen, Erik. "Bill Bradley's Game Plan." Institutional Investor. Vol. XCXI No. 2 (February, 1987): 69-80.

Johnson-Laird, P.N. and P.C. Wason, eds. Thinking: Readings in Cognitive Science. London: Cambridge University Press, 1977.

Johnson-Laird, P.N. Mental Models: Towards a Cognitive Science of Language, Inference and Consciousness. Cambridge, Massachusetts: Harvard University Press, 1983.

Kahler, Miles ed. The Politics of International Debt. Ithaca: Cornell University Press, 1986.

Kahneman, Daniel, Paul Slovic and Amos Tversky. Judgment Under Uncertainty: Heuristics and Biases. Cambridge,

Cambridge University Pres, 1982.

Kapur, Ishan. "An Analysis of the Supply of Euro-currency Finance to Developing Countries." IMF Exchange and Trade Relations Department (December 1976): 1-25.

Killick, Tony ed. <u>Adjustment and Financing in the Developing World</u>. Washington, D.C.: The International Monetary Fund, 1982.

Kindleberger, Charles. <u>Manias, Panics and Crises.</u> New York: Basic Books, 1978.

Kuipers, Benjamin J. "Representing Knowledge for Representation." In <u>Representation and Understanding,</u> edited by D. Bobrow and A. Collins, New York: Academic Press, 1975.

Kuttner, Robert. "Third World Debt: A Flawed Solution." <u>Business Week</u> , 19 January, 1987,
p. 18.

Lemgruber, Antonio Carlos, "New Directions in LDC Debt." Business ERconomics Vol. XXII No. 1 (January 1987): 22-25.

Lenat, Douglas B. "The Nature of Heuristics." <u>Artificial Intelligence</u> 19 (1981): 189-249.

Lessard, Donald R., and John Williamson. "Financial Intermediation Beyond the Debt Crisis." <u>Policy Analyses in International Economics. 12</u> Washington, D.C.: Institute for International Economics, 1985.

Lever, Harold and Christopher Huhne. <u>Debt and Danger: The World Financial Crisis.</u> Boston: The Atlantic Monthy Press, 1986.

Majeski, Stephen. "A Recommendation Model of War Initiation:

The Plausibility and Generalizability of General Cultural Rules." In Artificial Intelligence and National Security, edited by Stephen Cimbala. Lexington, Massachusetts: Lexington Books, 1987.

Marton, Andrew. "The Debate over Debt-for-Equity Swaps." Institutional Investor Vol. XXI No. 2 (February 1987): 177-180.

Mayer, Emilio. International Lending: Country Risk Analysis. Reston, Virginia: Reston Publishing Co., 1985.

McDonald, Robert. International Syndicated Loans. London: Euromoney Publications, 1983.

Minsky, Marvin. "A Framework for Representing Knowledge." In The Psychology of Computer Vision, edited by Patrick Henry Winston, New York: McGraw Hill, 1975.

Netto, Antonio Delfin. "Perspectives on the Adjustment Process: The Role of the Private Sector, the Euromarkets and the Adjusting Nations." Remarks Prepared for Presenation at the Annual Meeting of the International Monetary Conference, Lausanne, Switzerland,
2-5 June, 198.

Newell, Allen. "On the Analysis of Human Problem-Solving Protocals." In Thinking: Readings in Cognitive Science, edited by P.N. Johnson-Laird and P.C. Wason, London: Cambridge University Press, 1977.

_________, "Production Systems: Models of Control Structures." In Visual Information Processing by William Chase. New York: Academic Press, 1973.

Newman, Jay. "LDC Debt: The Secondary Market, the Banks and

New Investment in Developing Countries." Columbia Journal of World Business. Vol. XXI No. 3 (Fall 1986): 69-72.

Ollard, William. "The Debt Swappers." Euromoney (August 1986): 67-75.

Pecchiolo, R.M. The Internationalization of Banking: The Policy Issues. Geveva: Organization for Economic Cooperation and Development, 1984.

Phillips, Warren. "Alternative Futures in the Middle East: The Results from Three Simulations." In Artificial Intelligence and National Security, edited by Stephen Cimbala. Lexington, Massachusetts: Lexington Books, 1987.

Pylyshyn, Zenon. Compuation and Cognition: Toward a Foundation for Cognitive Science. Cambridge, Massachusetts: MIT Press, 1984.

Rieger, Chuck. "A System for Cause-Effect Representation and Simulation for Computer Aided Design." In Artificial Intelligence and Pattern Recognition in Computer Aided Design, edited by L. Latombe, New York: North Holland Publishing Company, 1978.

____ ."One System for Two Tasks: A CSA Memory that Solves Problems and Comprehends Language." University of Maryland, Department of Computer Science, TR-435, 1976.

____. "Spontaneous Computation in Cognitive Models." University of Maryland, Department of Computer Science, TR-459, 1976.

Rieger, Chuck and Milt Grinberg. "The Causal Representation and Simulation of Physical Mechanisms." University of Maryland, Department of Computer Science, TR-495, 1976.

Sachs, Jeffrey. "A New Approach to Managing the Debt Crisis." Columbia Journal of World Business. Vol. XXI No. 3 (Fall 1986): 41-49.

Schank, Roger C. and Robert Abelson. "Scripts, Plans and Knowledge." Proceedings of the Fourth International

Schrodt, Philip A. Pattern Matching, Set Prediction and Foreign Policy Analysis." In Artificial Intelligence and National Security, edited by Stephen Cimbala. Lexington, Massachusetts: Lexington Books, 1987.

Schubert, Martin. "Trading Debt for Equity." The Banker Vol. 137 No. 732 (February 1987): 18-20.

Simon, Herbert and Joseph Kadare. "Optimal Problem-Solving: Search-All or None Solutions." Artificial Intelligence 6 (1975): 235-247.

Smith, Gordon W., and John T. Cuddington. International Debt and the Developing Countries: A World Bank Symposium.

Stewart, Frances. "The International Debt Situation and North-South Relations." World Development 13 No. 2 (1985): 191-204.

Sylvan, Donald and Steve Chan. Foreign Policy Decision Making: Perception, Cognition and Artificial Intelligence. New York: Praeger Publishers, 1984.

Taylor, C.C. and M. Hudson. World Handbook of Social and Political Indicators. New Haven: YAle University Press, 1972.

The New Republic, "Better than Baker." (July 28, 1986): 9.

Thorson, Stuart and Kristi Anderson. "Computational Models, Expert Systems and Foreign Policy." In Artificial Intelligence and National Security, edited by Stephen Cimbala. Lexington, Massachusetts: Lexington Books, 1987.

Thorson, Stuart. "Intentional Inferencing in Foreign Policy: An AI Approach." In Foreign Policy Decision Making, edited by Donald Sylvan and Steve Chan. New York: Praeger Publishers, 1984.

Thorson, Stuart and Donald Sylvan. "Counterfactuals and the Cuban Missile Crisis." International Studies Quarterly 20 (1982): 529-571.

Treasury News. Various Issues.

Tversky, Amos and Daniel Kahneman. "Judgment Under Uncertainty: Heuristics and Biases." Science 185 (1974): 1124-1131.

Tversky, Amos and Daniel Kahneman. "The Framing of Decisions and the Psychology of Choice. Science 211 (1981): 453-458.

United Nations Economic and Social Council on Transnational Corporations. "Transnational Banks: Operations, Strategies and Their Effects in Developing Countries." Report of the Secretariat. E/C.10/67 10 April 1981.

United States Congressional Summit on Debt and Trade. New York, 1986.

U.S. Congress, Senate Committee on Foreign Relations, 1977.

International Debt, the Banks and U.S. Foreign Policy. Prepared by Karen Lissakers, 95th Congress, 1st Session, Washington, D.C.

Volker, Paul. "Illustrative Calculations of Examples of Hypothetical Debt Relief." Federal Reserve, Unpublished Paper, 1986.

Waterman, D.A. and A. Newell. "Protocal Analysis as a Task for Artificial Intelligence." Artificial Intelligence 2 (1971): 285-318.

Winograd, Terry. "Frame Representations and the Declarative-Procedural Controversy." In Representation and Understanding, edited by D. Bobrow and A. Collins, New York: Academic Press, 1975.

Winograd, Terry and Fernando Flores, Understanding Computers and Cognition: A New Foundation for Design. Norwood, New Jersey: Ablex Publishing Co., 1986.

Wolfgram, Deborah, Teresa Dear and Craig Galbraith. Expert Systems for the Technical Professional. New York: John Wiley and Sons, 1987.

World Bank, Development and Debt Service: Dilemna's of the 1980's. Washington, D.C.: The World Bank, 1986.

World Bank, Financing Adjustment with Growth in Sub-Saharan Africa, 1986-1990. Washington, D.C.: The World Bank, 1986.

World Bank, World Development Reports 1978-1987. New York: Oxford University Press.

World Financial Markets, "The Baker Initiative: The Perspective of the Banks." (February 1986): 1-14.

________, "International Bank Lending Trends." (July 1985): 1-11.

________, LDC Dect: Debt Relief or Market Solutions." (September 1986): 1-23.

________, "Strengthening the LDC Debt Strategy." (September/October 1985): 1-17.

INDEX

For Product Safety Concerns and Information please contact our EU representative GPSR@taylorandfrancis.com
Taylor & Francis Verlag GmbH, Kaufingerstraße 24, 80331 München, Germany

www.ingramcontent.com/pod-product-compliance
Lightning Source LLC
LaVergne TN
LVHW021113300926
849160LV00009B/712

* 9 7 8 1 1 3 8 8 6 5 6 4 8 *